FALLEN FEATHER

Deborah Chavez

Fallen Feather: a Spiritual Odyssey copyright pending, 1997 by Deborah Chavez. All rights reserved. Printed in the United States of America. No part of this book may be used or reproduced in any manner whatsoever without permission except in the case of quotations embodied in articles, books and reviews. For information, address;

Four Directions Publishing

P.O. Box 24671, Minneapolis, MN 55424
Phone: 612-922-9322, Fax 612-922-7163
E-mail: eagleman4@aol.com
Website: http://members.aol.com:/eagleman4

First Edition

Cover illustration by Ron Edwards.
Project Coordinator - Michael Poquette

DEDICATION

This is dedicated to Shane's two sisters
who survived their turbulent adolescence
and have become two powerful women,
each in their own way.

I want to thank Shane's oldest sister, for taking the risk in reaching out for help. If it were not for her, I would not be the person who I am today.

Without Shane this book would not exist. He wanted us to understand his struggle, as a teenager and as a Native American. He taught me many life lessons and I am deeply indebted to him.

As in all books, many people support the writer to complete the finished product. Sometimes I viewed it as pressure, other times gentle nudges, but it all helped me to get this into print. Certain individuals have been my rock to lean on through this long, sometimes tedious labor - my father, who always had the faith that I would finish this. My husband, Alan, who didn't grumble when I rehashed past events, wondering if anyone would really want to hear this story; yet understood my drive in completing the book. Ed McGaa, (Eagle Man) who cultivated the seedling in my mind, gave it a good watering when I'd forgotten to nourish it, and helped the flower to blossom. And Tom, my unwavering, dependable friend, who completely understood my love and dedication for Shane.

Helen, my editor, who had the tedious task of unscrambling my thoughts and decoding my meaning behind the words, I am forever grateful. Ron Edwards, who searched his heart and memories for the artistic cover, thank you.

Thank you to all who I haven't mentioned; you know who you are...

Contents

	Readers Note	3
1	"Secrets"	5
2	The Human Encounter	25
3	The "Res"	37
4	New Beginnings	45
5	Home to Roost	57
6	A Rose By Any Other Name	65
7	State of Confusion	71
8	Distancing	85
9	Nature Connection	97
10	The Pipe	113
11	The Reading	129
12	Dark Side of the Soul	137
13	Wrathful Eagle	143
14	Questions Unanswered	157
15	Epilogue	163
	Notes	177
	Suggested Readings	181

Readers Note

The names in this book have been altered. Because this story is true, confidentiality of the individual's involved in Shane's life was of my utmost concern.

Throughout this book you will notice that I refer to Shane as Sioux. The word Sioux was used to describe his Lakota tribe by the French. Although some may find this term insulting, Shane insisted upon my calling him Sioux, so I am respecting his wishes. Shane wasn't as adamant about the label applied to his ethnic group, so I use the terms Native American and American Indian as I deem appropriate.

1

"Secrets"

> "Come to the edge, he said.
> They said, 'We are afarid."
> Come to the edge, he said.
> They came.
> It pushed them . . .
> And they flew."
>
> Guillaume Apollinaire[1]

I STILL REMEMBER MY INTERVIEW FOR COLLEGE INTERNSHIP AT THE women's shelter. The address was supposed to be kept secret, although I found out that all the abusers in the Twin Cities knew where the shelter was. It took me five minutes to find a parking space on the residential street leading off one of the busiest streets in Minneapolis. I'm not going to say which street just in case one of those abusers has lost the address.

The shelter sat on the Mason-Dixon line; between the Native American and the Black American neighborhoods. It was actually two early 1900's renovated houses (back in the early 1980's the state sold condemned houses for a dollar, and one of these houses had been bought for a dollar). The houses were unattractive, somewhat dilapidated, and

6 "Secrets"

couldn't accommodate the thirty to forty women, children, and staff members who flowed in and out of them.

The place was surrounded by a five-foot black iron fence—like those fences in Dracula movies with the spear-like points on each post. Pushing open the iron gate, I glanced up at the three-story beige stucco house and saw bars over every single window. That made me a little nervous, and I peered back at my car, wondering if, in my pre-interview jitters, I had remembered to lock the doors. I climbed the porch steps and stood by the front door. It was painted an outrageous orange, and was one of those thick, steel fire doors with a small peep-hole—no windows whatsoever. There was an intercom and doorbell next to the knob, so I rang the bell a few times to make sure someone would hear it (I could hear kids crying somewhere inside). A few minutes passed and nothing happened. I felt as if a hundred eyes were on me, and abusers were waiting to jump on me at any second, so I rang the bell again, and again. Finally, a young female voice yelled from the intercom, "Yeah, wadda'ya want?"

I explained myself as quickly as I could, fearing she would cut me off and tell me to go away. "Just a minute," the voice snarled, and the intercom clicked off. I waited again. I was beginning to feel like Dorothy in the *Wizard of Oz*.

I rang the bell again and another, softer voice asked, "Yes?"

I repeated myself, but not as pleasantly as before, thinking I might be making a mistake about even considering interning at this place. Then I heard a half-dozen clicks as bolts were released, and a young woman opened the door. She slid the chain lock off and beckoned me inside, saying, "Wait here and I'll get the program director."

I stood in the foyer—well, maybe at the turn of the century it was a foyer. Now it was a dark, dank hallway with stained oak stairs leading up into darkness and a fluorescent light giving the place a sickeningly green tint. I considered leaving, but I was afraid an alarm would go off if I opened the door. The interview wasn't exactly what I had expected. I helped Barbara, the children's program director, move a couch from her office to the kids' room while she asked me questions about myself and my degree program. We settled on a starting date, and thus laid the ground for my career in psychology.

At 24 years old, I was a rookie when it came to knowledge of domestic abuse. According to Gail Sheehy's description of Baby Boomers in *New Passages* [2], I was born in the Me generation (1956-65), and, am embarrassed to say, had many of the traits she associated with that generation. Madonna's hit song, Material Girl, was one of my favorite's, describing my attitudes and snubbing the '60's hippies. I watched Wall Street ruled by power hitters in their 20's; as the first generation exposed to talk shows, I felt I could accomplish anything I wanted, with or without experience. If I played the correct role, wore the appropriate designer clothes, and accumulated the status-recognized material, I, too, could have it all. I had abnormally high expectations for myself and the world.

As a college student, I was in the majority. This was common for women in my generation. I didn't look at marriage as an escape route as my female predecessors had; I knew marriage was not essential for happiness or survival. Women did not need to be subservient to men. My parents battled a divorce with each other and subsequent marriages. I was very wary about the marriage institution. As characteristic of the Me's, I found it easier to live in the moment, with minimal demands and restraints on my emotions. As one person described the 'eighties in *New Passages* [3] "nothing was expected of you". I'm not proud in labeling myself in this category, although in those days I would have argued that point.

What pulled me into an internship at the shelter, besides altruistic tendencies, was a promise to myself of returning help I had received when I had been raped. The compassion and nurturance I received from complete strangers had touched me deeply, so I made a commitment to myself to offer the help I received to others in need. I wasn't ready to work with rape victims because my emotional wounds hadn't fully healed; so I chose work in a related field addressing the oppression of women.

I quickly learned about the subtle manipulation that destroys a person's self esteem by listening to the battered women describe the pain and suffering inflicted upon them repeatedly. My inexperience led me to ask myself, 'why do they stay?' Luckily, I never asked a battered woman that question. Instead, the women showed me hundreds of reasons why they stayed. It takes a strong, determined woman to leave her abuser. It isn't that easy to leave someone who has been supporting you and your children financially (and sometimes emotionally).

The children I worked with were confused and very angry with their mothers and their abusers—confused about the underlying reasons for the abuse and angry because their mothers weren't preventing the abuse, and so the abuse continued. I addressed these emotions through education and support groups, by reaching into their hearts and helping them feel their pain.

It was a normal Wednesday evening at the battered women's shelter. I always facilitated Kid's Group at seven o'clock on Wednesdays, no matter whether one child or twenty showed up. The shelter was full that night—fifteen women with children of all ages. I thought I'd have at least five school-age kids show up, partly because their moms would be in Women's Group, and there was nothing else for the kids to do except hang out. The children were new arrivals, so I prepared my standard first nighter's group agenda: "Why do women stay with abusive partners," and "No-one deserves to be hit." It took up the entire hour-and-a-half; and still kids left the group feeling that sometimes they and their moms deserved to be hit ("... but she asked for it...." is a typical comment). It was a tough message to get across to adults, but with children it was a little easier. That's why I chose to specialize in children—they're much more receptive to change and new ideas.

Even though most of the time my job was stressful, I really enjoyed the challenge and constant demand for action or reaction. (A lot of advocates describe working at a battered women's shelter as similar to working in an emergency room—you never know who will arrive or what will happen from one moment to the next.) I interned at this inner-city shelter as part of my Bachelor's degree program. After graduation, I was hired as a children's advocate and trained in sexual and physical abuse assessment, along with child development. My job consisted of screening children for physical, sexual, and emotional abuse, teaching mothers about parenting, and training children how to protect themselves. Children arrived at the shelter with their mothers under extremely stressful circumstances. Often they would arrive with only the clothes they were wearing, because the mother had been forced to make a quick getaway before her abuser discovered them missing.

It was time for group, and the women's advocates (women who specialize in working with battered women) shepherded the kids upstairs. The women's advocates looked forward to Kids' Groups because it gave them a respite from the hyperactivity of all those children running around the house. Group began with introducing ourselves one by one and stating why we were there. It seemed redundant, but a lot of kids were in denial about the real reasons why they were staying at a women's shelter. For many children, actually admitting that their mother was physically, sexually, or verbally abused destroyed their illusion of a normal happy family. It was difficult for me to understand this when I first began working with the kids, but as I listened to incident after incident of violence and degradation, I empathized with the children's need to idealize the situation. The mothers are often emotionally unable to discuss this with their children, so we started group by stating the obvious.

A new family had moved into the shelter the previous Sunday. The family members were Native Americans—Sioux—originally from North Dakota, but had lived in the city off and on for about five years. Marlina, the mother, had left her home in the middle of the night after a severe beating from her boyfriend, Len. She had taken her children with her—Shane aged thirteen and his two sisters, Allana aged ten and Missy aged nine. The children were withdrawn, but that was common for children during their first few days at the shelter.

By Tuesday Allana and Missy were visiting the play area and beginning to feel comfortable with me. Shane avoided all the children's advocates and followed his mother around the house. This is common for male children to play the role of protector, probably feeling responsible for his mother's abuse. I wanted to alleviate his fears, but whenever I entered the room, he would leave. He reminded me of a skittish rabbit. Rather than push the issue and risk alienating him, I decided to wait until he came to me. If he wanted to talk, I knew he'd eventually approach me.

I had a mixed group that night: Allana, Missy, and Shane (I had put the word out in the shelter that Shane had to show his face at group, but I really didn't expect him to show up), and two brothers - Lew aged nine, and Clarence, who was fourteen. Group was held upstairs in one of three rooms in the renovated attic. The surroundings left much to be desired, and most of the kid's didn't want to go up there without an adult. It was dark. Creaks and groans echoed throughout the rooms of the old house.

A few kids greeted me at the first-floor landing, and we trampled up two flights of narrow stairs to the third floor. As I flipped on the light, I was shocked to see Shane sitting on the floor. Concealing my surprise, I gathered the materials we needed for group and introduced myself.

I began by letting the kids make their own group rules and consequences. This way I wasn't assuming a controlling position and remained a mediator; also the kids felt that the group was their own. We talked about confidentiality and agreed on the rule, " What's said in the room stays in the room." Allana began questioning how much the adults were told about information revealed during children's group; she was overly concerned about confidentiality. I emphasized that everyone needed to feel free to express problems and concerns about their families. If one of the group members gossiped to an adult or to another kid, we would have to terminate the group. Shane sat at the back of the room, his eyes closed feigning sleep. I could tell he heard me because he nodded his head when I asked his sisters questions.

They were a quiet brood until we started to talk about the reasons women stay in abusive relationships. It dawned upon them that their mothers, even though they loved them, couldn't leave because of financial, family, and religious reasons, having nowhere to go, being brainwashed . . . We brainstormed up to fifty reasons on 'Why their mother stays'.

I could understand their frustration over why their mothers stayed with abusive partners. Adults have asked me thousands of times, "But why does she stay when he hits, or rapes, or threatens her?"

I explained, "When the person you love looks into your eyes and says, 'I'm sorry, I love you and I'll never do it again,' you want to believe with all your heart and soul that they are telling the truth, and you stay."

Once the kids had grasped most of the information I was giving them, a silence came over the group. I could see by their deep frowns and introspective gazes that they were processing a flood of memories about the abuse they had witnessed. Lew and Clarence were able to verbalize their feelings, and told about the most recent abusive incident. Allana tried to talk but kept getting interrupted by Lew. Missy frowned, not saying anything; and Shane, glaring at Allana, crossed his arms in front of his chest.

Toward the end of group Shane began to get bored and started playing around with the other boys. His sisters hung onto every word and participated fully. I could tell that, of all the children, Shane was the one I'd have the most trouble reaching. He was distant, remote, and sent a strong message that he wanted to be left alone. His body resembled a shield that deflected adults. The only words he uttered throughout the group were, "When's group ending?" and "Can we go now?"

When I focused the attention onto him, he'd slink further into the shadowy corner of the room and shrug his shoulders.

He was a good-looking boy, tall for his age, with shiny black hair that remind me of a midnight blue, and a dazzling smile that he used only once that evening—when I announced that group was over. He was all arms and legs, typical for his age, but his eyes . . . I saw in his eyes a glimpse of the pain and sorrow buried deep within his soul. Although he tried to hide this from adults, he was still a child, vulnerable. And he knew it. His face was a cold, emotionless mask, with a thin-lined scar vertical to his eye and cheek. That mask protected the secrets he stored inside his heart.

His sisters, on the other hand, were giggly and fun to be around. Missy, the entertainer, was very outgoing and verbal. She immediately closed down, though, when we talked about physical abuse towards women. Allana was an observer, absorbing the activity and dynamics

12   "Secrets"

of the others, but rarely interacted with them. Missy would occasionally pull Allana's arm to get her sister involved, but Allana would remove herself from the conversation as quickly as she could, without drawing attention to herself. There seemed to be a dark cloud of secrets over these children, but they didn't trust me, so I approached them with trepidation.

The group came to a close with my asking the kids if someone ever deserves to be hit. The group unanimously agreed that no one should be hit, not even kids. Some hinted about abuse from their dads or older siblings, but time was running out, so I didn't delve into it. I made a mental note to pursue this on an individual basis, and ended. Shane pushed us out of the way and bolted from the room. Lew and Clarence followed, play wrestling; Allana and Missy helped me straighten the room.

Missy brought some materials downstairs for me, and I began the tedious job of charting my observations in their files. Allana was hovering by the door, waiting for something. Sensing that she wanted to talk to me, I shuffled some papers, avoiding eye contact. I asked her what she thought of the group, and she muttered, "Okay."

She asked some vague questions about confidentiality, "Did I ever tell a parent what a child said? Did I ever tell the police what a child said?"

I explained that my job was to protect children, and if a child was in danger, then an agency called Child Protection Services would help me to protect the child. I asked her if she was in danger. She looked away, holding back the tears.

"My mother's been beating me up the whole time we've been staying at the shelter. I thought this place was supposed to protect kids too," Allana cried out.

Hitting children was against house rules, and mothers were asked to leave if they didn't abide by those rules. Of course, Allana was aware of this rule. "Are you going to kick us out? We don't have anywhere else to go. And if my mom finds out, she'll beat me up so bad . . . I'm afraid, please don't tell her—please!"

"Allana, when was the last time she beat you up?" I asked her quietly.

"Right before group. Shane, Missy and me were walking with my mom to the store. Everything was fine until we started to walk back to the shelter. My mom suddenly goes nuts and starts punching me. I screamed at her, 'Don't you touch me, leave me alone', but she grabbed my hair, threw me down on the sidewalk and dragged me by my hair. Look at my eyes. She made me wear this blue stuff so you wouldn't be able to see my eyes." Allana smeared the blue eye shadow with her knuckles, revealing a shiner on her right eye.

"What else happened, Allana?" I asked. Working with children, I had learned that there was always more; children expect adults to ask for more information before they continue. Crying hysterically, she told me she was so afraid I would yell at her, or worse, tell her mom.

"Mom told me I'd get a worse beating than just the black eye if I told anyone, especially the people working at the shelter." The two main rules at the shelter are that physical abuse of children is not permitted, and that children must never be left unsupervised. Breaking those two rules results in immediate eviction of the woman and her children.

Allana wanted me to swear that I wouldn't tell a soul about the incident, but, as a helping professional, I was mandated by law to report any knowledge of child abuse—physical or sexual—to Child Protection Services (CPS). What may appear as an easy decision is very emotional when it involves the trust of a child. I knew the child welfare system had failed to protect and defend children in the past, due to legal boundaries and human error. It was very difficult for me to look in Allana's innocent face and try to explain the consequences of her actions. How could I protect Allana from further abuse and continue to foster her trust in helping professionals while meeting the legal requirements of my profession?

After calming her, I explained how Child Protection works to help children and why I had to tell them what she had told me. But I promised Allana that neither I nor CPS would tell her mother that she had confided in me. We hugged, and Allana went skipping down the stairs, relieved of her dark secret. I, however, knew that the future was far from rosy for her. The promise I made to Allana depended upon the sympathy of the CPS worker; I had no power over that person, and

14 "Secrets"

the CPS worker could easily dismiss my wishes. I was determined to make things right for Allana, she had taken a very big risk in revealing this information, and, regardless of the outcome, her life would never be the same again.

I sat in that room a long time, wondering how I could even begin to help her. If I reported the abuse to CPS, Marlina would eventually find out that her daughter had told me about it. If I didn't report it, the abuse would never be discovered, and I certainly didn't have any power over her mother to supervise her parenting.

Marlina had been living on the streets of Minneapolis, and her daily activities included drinking and using drugs. Although only twenty-nine years old, she appeared to be in her late forties. Her build was small and stocky; her skin, which was yellowed from jaundice, sagged on her bones. She had led a very difficult and troubled life. According to her intake form, she had stabbed another woman in a bar brawl a few months earlier, and she had a history of abuse—both as a victim and a perpetrator. She admitted to a violent temper and chemical dependency. Leaving an abusive relationship in Michigan, Marlina had chosen Minneapolis to be among her relatives, but had no permanent address. I had no choice: CPS had to intervene in this family before one of the children got killed. I made my report to CPS, stressing repeatedly that further abuse of Allana was highly likely, so caution had to be exercised. A social worker would interview her at school the following day, and would call me back to confirm and corroborate the report. Luckily, Marlina was out of the shelter for the day, so I didn't have to face her. I could not have looked her in the eye without revealing my disgust and contempt for her behavior.

I wasn't sure how Allana would react to me now: sometimes kids avoided me after revealing incidents of abuse. Shame, guilt, and remorse would cloud over them and render them helpless. Two weeks earlier, a child had revealed to me that his mother physically abused him; then admitted to his mother that he had broken their secret. The next day the family disappeared from the shelter, the mother probably fearing that her children would be taken away from her. In reality, this rarely happened, unless the parent refused psychological treatment for the abusive behavior.

Allana sought me out in the playroom as soon as she came home from school. We sat together on cushions on the floor, and I began to explain what I had done. She looked horrified and her first words were, "My mother will find me and beat me."

I assured her that she was safe at the shelter, and I would do everything I could to protect her. When I asked her if her mother suspected anything, Allana said she didn't think so, but added that her mother had been watching her after she returned from group last night. I pointed out that we would have to be more careful in the future. Marlina was probably curious as to why Allana hadn't come down with the other kids after group.

Allana was nervous about talking to CPS and threatened to play hooky from school the next day. It was her choice, I explained, but that wouldn't stop her mother abusing her. Once her family left the shelter, I could no longer protect Allana. After a long silence, Allana agreed to the interview and promised to tell the social worker the truth, but only if her mother wouldn't find out.

The social worker interviewed Allana without her mother's permission. That was somewhat unusual; in those days, they investigated abuse by talking to the mother before talking to the child, but it was very apparent that Allana's life was in danger from her mother. I went through a day of anguish, wondering if the interview was successful. Quite often children become frightened after reporting abuse and recant their stories, which makes it virtually impossible to investigate the allegations.

Late that afternoon, Allana saw me as she was getting off the school bus. I was heading for my car, ready to call it a day. She gave me a bear hug and shyly handed me a handmade envelope. "Open it now, pleeeaase." It was addressed:

"To: A children avocate, Debby

          From: A kid, Allana"

Adorning the envelope were two overlaid hearts with streamers flowing from them, and paper cutouts of balloons were stapled to the ends of the streamers. Inside, a sheet of white paper folded in half was addressed the same way as the envelope, and she had drawn another heart with "love" written inside it. Allana had written:

16   "Secrets"

> *"You help me out when I fell in*
> *and now I am standing again.*
> *So I just wanted to say that I am happy*
> *for what you did Debby."*

The back of the folded page was painted with watercolors of green, blue, and pink. I was speechless and stunned, blinking back tears. I had never received such a warm, heartfelt gift before. I also felt guilty because I knew that her life as she knew it would drastically change as a direct result of this CPS report. Yet she trusted me to help and had hope I could change it. My fears and doubts evaporated as I looked into her eyes and told her that she was brave and would be okay She squeezed my hand and went running towards the gate of the shelter—a shelter that truly protected her.

Allana's case was in the investigative phase, so every day stretched into nightmare proportions as more shelter staff heard about the CPS report. The investigation was on hold until Marlina left the shelter, but they were monitoring her behavior. Allana was relatively safe living in the shelter, and CPS didn't want Marlina to suspect she was under investigation for fear that she would run off, leaving no forwarding address. Marlina was free to leave the shelter at any time.

The shelter was small—a staff of nine women's advocates and four children's advocates—and I knew that Marlina would eventually hear through the grapevine that a report had been made against her. Meanwhile, Allana began to hang around the kids' recreation room painting, making crafts, and playing games. Shane and Missy were never around the shelter, as Marlina took them with her. As the weekend approached, I began to feel apprehensive because I had Saturday and Sunday off. I briefed the weekend staff on the status of the investigation and tried to let go of my feelings of doom.

Eight o'clock on Sunday morning, the phone rang. Lounging, reading the newspaper, I wrestled over whether I should answer the it. On the fourth ring, the telephone won. It was Krissy, one of the women's advocates, notifying me that Marlina had abandoned her children. She had left the shelter at seven o'clock on Saturday evening and asked another resident to watch her children, promising to be back by nine.

The police would have to be called if Marlina didn't show up within the hour. Because of my previous involvement with the children, Krissy asked me if I would come to the shelter and explain the situation to the children, not a pleasant task to be doing on my day off.

As I made the ten minute drive to the shelter, I secretly hoped that Marlina wouldn't return: it would be a blessing in disguise for the children. CPS would have to intervene, and appropriate foster placement would be initiated for the children.

I arrived at the shelter just in time to see Allana, Missy, and Shane stumbling down the stairs, rubbing sleep out of their eyes. They were surprised to see me, knowing it was my day off, but they didn't ask where their mother was, and why she wasn't fixing them breakfast. I decided not to explain anything to them until I had talked to Krissy; and I distracted them with talk of what they wanted for breakfast and who was going to help prepare it. Shane grabbed a skillet and began preparing the sausages, Allana pulled out pancake mix, and Missy set the table. The kids chattered on about their school and Shane gossiped about a girl he was interested in. It was so much fun seeing the kids interacting like a family, and very obvious that they were starved for adult affection. Laughing and teasing each other, we cooked breakfast together. As the children sat down to eat pancakes, sausage, and eggs, Krissy and I went into the advocate's office, closing the door behind us.

"You know, I have to call the police pretty soon," she said quietly. I asked Krissy to let me prepare the children and not to call the police until after they had finished eating. She agreed, and I went back into the dining room.

"You guys know where your mom is?" I quizzed them. They shook their heads in response.

I reminded them of the rule about leaving kids alone overnight, and Missy exclaimed, "We're not alone, you're with us!"

I told her I wasn't her mother and described what would happen if their mother didn't come back within the hour. Shane tried to explain that she disappeared frequently but always returned back to them in a few days. I explained that they couldn't stay at the shelter without their mother: it was illegal and I could get into trouble. Allana came

18 "Secrets"

up with the idea that they could hide in the house and no one need see them until Marlina showed up. I told her it was impossible and not an option. Krissy had to call the police, who would take them to a safe place. Well, that went over like a lead balloon. Shane threw back his chair and ran into the TV room, Missy started crying, and Allana stared at me.

I gathered the children together again in the TV room. Shane violently kicked a chair while I tried to calm Missy. I told them, " I had no choice. Your mother knows the rules, and she didn't call to tell us where she is. I promise you'll be in a safe home where no one will hurt you, and I'll visit you every day."

I had no idea how I was going to visit them every day, with the full schedule of working and attending college; but I didn't want to abandon them also.

That seemed to calm them, and Shane suddenly smiled and suggested they go and pack their bags. The girls agreed, and I followed them upstairs. Missy asked me to help her pack. She was starting to cry again, so I followed her into their room, while Shane went to his. He slept in the room next to his mom and sisters.

We finished packing, then went downstairs and waited in the foyer for Shane. After a few minutes, I sent Allana upstairs to see if he was ready. She came running down, screaming, "He's gone, he's gone!".

I ran to his room, checking to see if he had taken his belongings. Everything was there, even his prized possession, his watch. The residents and advocates joined in a house search and found nothing except the back door standing wide open. Surprisingly, the girls didn't seem very concerned about Shane. When I commented on it, they told me he had probably run away to find their mom because he hated foster homes. Allana explained that Shane had been physically abused at more than one foster home.

I placed a missing person's report over the phone, but the police officer emphasized that if an adolescent didn't want to be found, they wouldn't find him. He hinted that Shane had probably gone to his mother, and that if he was on the run, the Native American community would never reveal his location to the police. I hung up feeling frustrated, thinking that if Shane had been a rich white boy, the police reaction would have been different.

The residents and staff of the shelter began a boy hunt. The women canvassed the neighborhood on foot, checking the alleys; the school-age kids went on bikes to check out local parks and playgrounds; the women's advocates got on the phone and spread the word throughout Shane's community that he had run away and to please contact the shelter.

Meanwhile, Clarence, who had been at the children's group the other night, took me to Shane's secret hideouts, including a seedy pool hall. On one of the most dangerous street corners in the city, a flight of stairs led to a blacked-out door with broken windows. I made Clarence wait in the car, even though he insisted that he went there all the time with Shane, and it was safe. I tiptoed up the stairs, heart pounding a mile a minute, worrying that I'd open that door and be threatened, or worse case, attacked.

Actually, it wasn't that bad—just billiard tables crammed into a rank, smoky room. Besides a kid who looked Shane's age managing the place, I was the only person there. I described Shane's features, asking the kid if he'd seen him today. He shook his head, saying he hadn't seen Shane for a few days. Then he rambled on about Shane being a bad ass pool hustler and always winning money. Obviously Shane wasn't as innocent as I had previously thought.

Clarence and I checked out a few more places, then rejoined the rest of the search party. No luck. We had exhausted all of our possibilities. Shane had disappeared into the city. My only hope was that he had found his mother and was staying with her rather than living on the street. At least he'd be safe. I had betrayed the small amount of trust he had in me and I assumed I would never hear from him again. Feeling faint from emotional exhaustion, I looked at my watch. We'd been looking for Shane for over four hours. I asked the girls if they were hungry.

Allana, Missy, and I went to lunch, and as we ate, we talked about their mother. They shed light on why they didn't want to go into a foster home. Marlina had recently taken the children out of foster care in North Dakota and brought them to Minneapolis to live with her. At first the kids had been excited, looking forward to a fresh beginning with their mother. Unfortunately, soon after they arrived, Marlina had met her abuser and began drinking heavily and using drugs. It was common for the kids to be at home alone, sometimes for a week at a time. Luckily their relatives had lived down the block, so they frequently stayed overnight with them.

The girls were two years behind in school, Shane four years. I asked them why Shane was so far behind, and they explained that he had been placed separately in foster homes and had continually run away from them. I started to get the feeling that these kids were never with their mother for any length of time, and Allana verified that fact. During her short life, she had spent a total of one year with her mother. The rest of her years had been spent in foster care or with relatives on the reservation. Missy admitted that the short time she had spent with Marlina hadn't been very pleasant.

I asked the girls what had been their worst foster care experience. Allana looked at Missy, then back at me. Staring at her plate, Allana began telling me about Missy's uncle who had abused her when she was six years old. Allana had witnessed it, narrowly escaping the abuse herself by pretending she was asleep. Missy quietly played with her food as Allana talked. "Missy, how did you feel when that happened?" I asked.

Okay," she shrugged.

"Okay? Missy, come on now. You were hurt and scared. You can't tell me you were okay ."

"Well, maybe not, but I don't remember and I'm fine now," she answered abruptly. I didn't push her. I didn't want to open another can of worms—there were so many crawling around already.

I asked if anything else had happened to them. "There was that time Shane was locked in the closet for a few days," Allana casually replied. I encouraged her to continue, under Missy's suspicious, watchful eye.

"We were staying with these mean old people, they made us call them Grandma and Grandpa, but we weren't related. They'd leave us for days at a time, but they didn't trust Shane 'cause Shane would threaten to run away and tell. So they'd lock him up in their bedroom closet, and lock us up in the other bedroom. But Shane figured out a way to escape, so he set us free and we ran away."

I wanted to continue unearthing the girls' secrets and help them release some of this garbage they had stored in their hearts, but I was overwhelmed with my emotions. We finished eating and headed to the foster home. Surprisingly, the girls were in good spirits, laughing and singing along with the radio.

The foster home was in a beautiful, suburban neighborhood. An elderly white couple greeted us while the girls hung behind me, not making eye contact. While the girls unpacked their clothes, I briefed the foster parents on the situation, explaining the girl's previous foster home experiences. The couple was understanding and thanked me. Not wanting to abandon Allana and Missy, I stayed for a while and played a few board games with them. We talked about their favorite music, and slowly they began to relax . . . until it was time for me to go. They whimpered and begged me to stay overnight with them. They both knew that was impossible, but I couldn't blame them for trying. After promising I'd be back the next day, with their friends from the shelter, we exchanged hugs.

I had no memory of the drive back to my home. My nerves were raw. My emotions were numb. I didn't have the energy to worry whether the girls would run away from the foster home. I was past the point of emotional exhaustion.

I visited Allana and Missy the following afternoon and every afternoon until they left the foster home. In fact, nearly every adult and child at the shelter (including staff) visited them during the five days they stayed there. The children and I threw a going-away party for them on their last day. They were going back to their reservation in North Dakota, to live in a foster home. Their Sioux tribe assumed custody and jurisdiction over the children, including Shane, because Marlina had abandoned them. Luckily, Allana and Missy wanted to go back to the reservation: they had happy memories of life there and extended family to emotionally support them.

As I drove them to the airport, we talked about flying (it was their first time in a plane) and made small talk, trying to ease the tension.

"Secrets"

I couldn't help feeling depressed, thinking that somehow I had failed because only two children were returning. I played the "If only I had done . . . If only I had said . . " scenario until Allana jarred me back to my senses by saying that, thanks to me, she was going back to her land. Smiling, I hugged her and Missy. Then, before we all ended up crying, I shooed them onto their plane, where Flora, the Tribal Court Representative, was waiting to escort them.

I called Flora the following week to check up on the girls, secretly hoping she had heard from Marlina and knew of Shane's whereabouts. She didn't have any further information about Shane or Marlina, but the girls were adapting well and had a great foster mother. She did shed some light on Shane's background, saying he was "a very . . . should we say . . . industrious child."

At age ten, he had stolen a car and drove it from North Dakota to Minneapolis, Minnesota, which is over 400 miles. He had a long history of running and had been placed in numerous foster homes, always unsuccessfully. Flora hinted that he always took off looking for his mother, who would disappear into the bars of the nearby town. She told me to give up on Shane because we'd never hear from him again.

Marlina never contacted or returned to the shelter, but that was fairly common with alcoholics. I packed up her clothing and put them in a storage area.

As time passed, a kind of lethargy cloaked my feelings about Shane. But whenever his face or his name crept into my consciousness, a sense of foreboding nagged at me. I attributed it to the guilt for not having being able to help him and tried to shrug it off. I felt good about the situation with the girls, who had been placed in a wonderful foster home. They feared the wrath of their mother, but Marlina couldn't reclaim the children without facing a tribal court hearing.

The loose end was Shane. I never got close to him, and I'm sure he felt that I stole his sisters away from him. If only I could explain to him why I did what I did; talk to him, help him understand I'm not like the other people who had hurt him. Worried that a boy his age was running the streets with no money and no clothes, I wanted to do something—anything—but what? I chose this field because I wanted to save the children of the world.

I promised myself that if I could save just one person from a life of abuse and cruelty, I would be able to hold my head up high and understand why I was on this earth.
As Black Elk, a Holy Man of the Oglala Sioux, was quoted,

> *" ... man who has a vision*
> *is not able to use the power of it*
> *until he has performed the vision on earth*
> *for people to see."* [4]

Your problems pile up one by one

You won't deal with them

You just want to have some fun...

I know you're hurt

It's clear to see the pain and confusion

when you're with me

Please open your eyes

Don't be afraid

Seek the answer...

Please take my hand

For I'll be there

When life really hurts.

You know I care.

Don't ruin yourself

By taking the easy way out.

You may be very sorry

For the price you didn't pay.

No one can make you do it

You have to do it for you

But I'll give you hope, help, and reason

Because I love you.

Shane Lone Eagle, 1985

2

The Human Encounter

M Y EMPLOYMENT AT THE SHELTER CONTINUED TO EXPAND MY horizons and my awareness. As an employee, I was required to participate in homophobic workshops (fear of lesbians and gay men); anti-racism training; classism in-services (discrimination on the basis of socio-economic status); and ageism conferences (discrimination against older people). I was on the "front lines"—working at a shelter that serviced Blacks, Native Americans, Asians, Hispanics, and Whites from all socio-economic backgrounds. I had to learn how to accept people who were raised differently from me and be an advocate for them, thereby supporting their decisions regardless of my opinion. Sound easy? It was traumatic, painful soul-searching.

Going through this self-analysis jarred me into realizing that I was a member of a minority group, even though I passed for white in the white world. Because I had been raised by my mother and grandmother, who were German, and had blatantly ignored the fact that my father was full-blooded Mexican, I grew up thinking that I could seize any opportunity (opportunities for women, that is . . .). Of course, racist individuals would stare at me and exclaim that something about my facial features looked foreign. After asking my last name, they would assume I was French, because my last name was pronounced with a soft "Cha," as in Shaw.

Actually, my father changed the pronunciation in elementary school to avoid discrimination after his teacher told him his name didn't sound American. His brothers and sisters changed the spelling from Chavez to Chaves, but kept the Mexican pronunciation. Many people assumed I was an exotic French woman. When I told them I was Mexican, their reaction was predictable, "No, you can't be, you don't look Mexican!"

Now, why would anyone in her right mind say she was part of a minority if she wasn't? What advantage would I have? Being accepted by white people? No. Job advancement? No. I have never been able to understand it. As I learned more about racism, I realized I was fortunate to have been raised as I was—it opened more doors to me, although I lost much of my Mexican heritage.

I absorbed this education like a parched sponge suddenly swept into the sea. My mind reeled with all the new information, which I tried to incorporate into my life and eventually led me to change the way I related to people. As the old saying goes, you can't con a con; and believe me, you were instantly called on your garbage at the shelter.

It was one of those hot, muggy afternoons in Minnesota when you pray it will rain just to get relief from the humidity. The sky darkened, preparing for a thunderstorm. I was sitting in the kid's room with all the lights on, halfheartedly playing with two preschoolers, but thinking about our latest anti-racism training. I looked up when I heard the door close and saw a tall, gaunt boy standing in the shadows. Thinking it was one of the kids staying at the shelter, I beckoned to him, patting the chair beside me. As he came out of the darkness, I saw that it was Shane. My mouth opened, but I couldn't speak. My thoughts raced: 'Why is he here? Is his mom here? What should I do?' I didn't want to scare him away.

We made small talk and I tried to act as casually as I could, fearful that one wrong word would send him scurrying like a scared rabbit. He was very nervous, rarely glancing at me, fidgeting with the buttons on his shirt. Krissy barged into the room looking for a toy and did a double-take when she saw Shane. She stayed cool, acting as if she'd just seen him yesterday rather than two months ago. As they talked, I studied him out of the corner of my eye, without being obvious: his clothes were stained and dirty, and he was extremely thin with sunken cheeks. His shoes had holes in them, and his hair was matted, but his body was clean, at least I knew he had bathed recently.

Krissy offered him a plate of the snacks we kept on hand for the kids, and he ate hungrily as we scurried for juice. They talked a while longer until it was time for dinner. She invited him back, casually asking if he was staying close by. Shane said he was staying two blocks away with his mom and her boyfriend. I encouraged him to drop in, saying he was always welcome. Then Krissy and I watched him walk through the gate and down the street.

Shane came back the next morning, played with the kids, ate lunch, and left. I tried not to appear too excited to see him, yet didn't want to distance myself. I didn't want him to think I was angry he ran away. I was walking on eggshells with him and felt drained after every encounter. The shelter staff allowed him to hang around the house, and within a week he was spending up to twelve hours a day at the shelter. My supervisor, Barbara, pulled me over on the ninth day and made a proposition. If she could arrange for him to get paid for playing with the children and entertaining them (always under staff guidance), would I be willing to take the responsibility of supervising him?

This was like a dream come true. I could keep my eye on Shane with the expectation that he report to me everyday through the guise of being an employee. True, there was a fleeting question of boundaries; former resident with a history of unreliability working with abused children, but I was so deep into the trench of Shane's world that boundaries didn't concern me. I would do whatever was necessary to keep that boy from running away.

I rushed through the house, looking for Shane. He was watching television with some of the younger kids. When I offered him the chance to work with the children, he showed more enthusiasm than I had ever seen before, and asked when he could start.

"Right now", I replied.

He jumped up, gathered the kids, and began organizing a fishing trip to a nearby lake. I interrupted, asking how he was going to get all the kids to the lake, which was eight miles away. He looked at me shyly and asked if I would take them. My heart was shouting "YES!" but I said nonchalantly, "Yea, I suppose I could change my day around."

So, Shane became an official employee of the shelter, under the terms of some federal funding, and I could keep my eye on him, with a glimmer of hope that I might gain his trust.

The children's advocates celebrated the day Shane received his first paycheck. He got paid for twenty hours a week, even though he spent every day and evening, including weekends at the shelter. The children bonded with him and looked forward to his arrival each day. I think it was the first time in his life that someone actually cared where he was. He spent his first paycheck on clothes, but it didn't go very far. By the time he got his third paycheck, the women's advocates suggested we pass around the hat and pitch in some money for Shane's wardrobe. Krissy and I handed him seventy-five dollars, along with some hand-me-downs from the staff's children. Shane ran out of the room, overcome with emotion.

I felt proud as I watched how happy he was. I heard the stories of children seeking Shane out to talk with him about their feelings. For some reason I was drawn to him, although he was as skittish as a deer exposed by the headlights of a car. It was truly a case of living one day at a time. I was just happy that he had let me share this much of his life with him.

I watched Shane gain weight and begin to laugh and talk more as he played with the children. We all were amazed by the transformation and enjoyed being around him. Then, as quickly as he had blossomed, he deteriorated: his clothing became torn, his hair greasy, his gait faltering. I knew I had to talk to him even though it meant he might disappear again—perhaps forever. I was the adult closest to him—maybe too close, because I knew it would be painful for me if he ran away.

My heart pounding wildly, I cornered him in the playroom and asked him what was wrong. After a few seconds of stuttering and stalling, he burst out, "She's stealing my checks from me. She beats me up and takes them to buy booze and drugs, and she told me I'd better not say anything or she'd kill me." I asked who 'she' was.

"My mother", he yelled out.

I didn't know what to say. After hearing kids tell me that they've been beaten and sexually molested in every way imaginable, I was still capable of being shocked by the horror children have to endure with their parents. I think my attachment to Shane also contributed to my reaction, causing me to lose my sense of perspective.

In the end, I reacted as I had been trained to do, which is to show no strong reaction of shock or horror, but to be supportive and nurturing. I asked him what he wanted to do, knowing that if I suggested anything, he'd refuse the help. And I certainly wasn't going to bring up foster homes. Shane surprised me by saying he wanted to live with his sisters; he knew they were living in a foster home on the reservation. Still letting him take the lead, I asked him how I could help. He asked me to contact Flora, who would have to call a tribal hearing to request custody of him. That's when I had to tell him that the tribe already had custody of him because his mom had abandoned them at the shelter.

He lowered his head and nodded, but kept his thoughts to himself. I dreaded reminding him of that time, but knew I had to in order to clear the air between us and establish honest communication. Pretending that nothing had happened was something he and his mother had done repeatedly, and I wanted to role model healthier interactions, regardless of how it might strain our relationship.

I kept Shane in the room so he didn't think I was talking about him behind his back, as I placed the call to his tribe. I spoke to Flora, who was already familiar with the family. I updated her on Shane's latest encounter with his mother, and Shane's request to live with his sisters. She hesitated and asked why Shane wanted to come back to the reservation. I explained how he had been transformed during the short time he had worked at the shelter, and how, with the proper direction and nurturance, he could be a terrific kid. Shane was sitting next to me hearing all this, questioning me with a confused look, knowing something was wrong.

Again Flora hesitated, stammering, and then admitted that the tribe didn't want him back; he had a destructive history with them and they felt it wouldn't benefit anyone if Shane returned. Words can hardly express how I felt at that instant: stunned, overwhelmed by pain and sadness. I had been taught that the Native American tribes took care of their own people, so how could they turn away a young child who wanted to return?

Flora suggested I contact his mother's tribe (she didn't know which one, though) to see if he could live on that reservation. Without showing too much emotion, because Shane was watching me closely, I presented Shane's position. He had nowhere to live, he couldn't stay at the shelter, and there was a court order from the tribe stating that he was in their custody. She put me on hold, and my mind reeled. What was I going to do with Shane if they wouldn't take him? Child Protection Services wouldn't be able to help because he was in the tribe's custody. At best he'd be placed in a foster home—and I knew how he'd feel about that.

Shane, sensing danger, pulled away from the desk and walked into the other room. I wasn't concerned about him running away just then because he had nowhere to go. I was his last resort. Flora came back on the line and, very reluctantly, stated that Shane would be allowed to return if he agreed to behave appropriately—no more running away, and no contact with his mother. If he broke this agreement, he would be sent to a state orphanage. I called Shane to the phone, and Flora restated the tribe's demands. He agreed, and plans were made to send him back to the reservation in one week.

We had seven days until his departure. Meanwhile his mother had called twice while we were on the phone with Flora, somehow sensing that something was happening. She left messages that she was looking for him and wanted him to come home immediately. We sat at the desk in silence for a while. Then Shane asked if he could stay with me until it was time to leave. It was all I could do to stop myself from saying yes, but it was shelter policy that residents couldn't stay in the homes of staff, both for the welfare of the staff and the individual—so that appropriate boundaries could be maintained. It tore at my heart to explain this to him, but he nodded and became silent again.

Barbara walked in just then and, seeing the sorrow on our faces, asked what was wrong. I told her briefly, and she reiterated that Shane couldn't stay with me. I would be dismissed from the shelter, and she wouldn't be able to prevent it. She apologized and helped us brainstorm other possibilities. After a couple of dead ends, Shane remembered Eleanore, an aunt of his who lived a few miles from the shelter. His mom had fought with her, so he knew Eleanore would keep his whereabouts secret from his mother.

Since Aunt Eleanore didn't have a phone, I drove Shane to her house, which was in the Native American community. It wasn't far enough away from his mother for my liking. Shane asked me to wait in the car, so I watched anxiously as he walked up to the gate.

There were kids playing in the dirt yard, who stopped to stare at me every so often. I stood out not only because I was non-Indian but also because my car, a brand new ocean-blue two-seater sports car, was a Las Vegas showstopper. I enjoyed the attention I received from men most of the time, but right now I could have done with a more conservative car.

Fifteen minutes went by, and I began to get nervous. I worried that Aunt Eleanore could have called Marlina, not wanting to harbor her son, and was restraining Shane against his will. . . . As I tried to decide how much longer I would wait before going in, Shane trotted out, yelling, "It's okay, I can stay."

Still not trusting the situation, I kept asking, "You're sure, absolutely sure you're safe here?"

He looked at me wide-eyed, as if I was a crazed lunatic, patted my hand, and said calmly, "Yes Deb, I'll see you at work tomorrow," and, dropping his bag of clothes to the ground, ran off to play tag with his cousins.

I was ambivalent about his safe haven, knowing, in the Native American community, he wouldn't remain a secret for long. It was a temporary measure, at best. His mother called or visited the shelter five to ten times a day, threatening to contact the police if we didn't tell her where her son was staying. By some twist of fate, I never ran into her during this drama, even though she was staking out the shelter with her drinking cohorts. I heard all this from two Native American co-workers who had direct links to Marlina. Luckily no-one revealed Shane's location to her.

As the pressure built, my sources disclosed that Shane couldn't stay at his hideout for another night; they couldn't guarantee his safety. I called a meeting with my coworkers Richard and Krissy, and explained my predicament. Shane had to have a safe hideout for five days, and the only person who could provide that was me. I told them I was willing to risk losing my job to protect a child from harm and would take unpaid leave from the shelter until Shane was gone. Everyone supported me and offered any assistance they could.

Shane and I would stay at my home in St. Paul, where I was living with my dad. There was no way his mom could find us there. Richard would take Shane for this first night until I finished my shift the following day. Krissy would run interference, reporting Marlina's movements to me and covering my tracks. I reminded them of our supervisor's warning regarding immediate termination, and they all agreed that if I was fired, they would quit under protest because my actions were not on paid company time. I knew this was a weak argument, but it did alleviate my fears about jeopardizing my job long enough for me to concentrate on Shane.

As luck would have it, Barbara walked in on our meeting just as we were congratulating ourselves on our cunningness. She studied our faces and said, "I know you're up to something, and it involves Shane, but I don't want to know anything until it's all over."

She then looked at me and said, "Deborah, I trust your judgment in this."

'God, if she only knew ', I thought. After it was all over, I learned she had overheard our conversation.

Our plan worked perfectly, and Shane had a pretty good time of it. My dad wasn't too excited about hiding someone's child, even under these circumstances. Actually, he had adamantly refused at first, but, as manipulative as I had been throughout this process, I wasn't going to let one person's refusal stop me. I knew that once he met Shane, he feelings would melt, so I brought him home the next day and began preparing dinner. My dad never mentioned that I'd disobeyed his wishes (I was staying at his house temporarily until my home loan went through, so I was pushing it), but he was somewhat quiet and stern for the first few hours. Then, as I had predicted, he couldn't help but love Shane.

I wanted to make those days special for Shane, so we went to the zoo and saw movies. I tried to fulfill some of his childhood wishes. We ate junk food, and I played like a kid again, releasing a lot of my stress and tension.

But it wasn't all fun and games. Krissy called me two or three times a day, keeping me posted on Marlina's progress. His mother had decided it wasn't wise to call the police. Instead, she told the shelter staff that she knew I was the one responsible for turning her son away from her, and said she had ordered a 'hit' on me. She hung about with some sleazy people who had offered to kill me for a price. I didn't move in Marlina's circles, so, although I was apprehensive, I felt fairly safe. Shane took it much more seriously than I did (he had heard about the hit through other shelter staff) and was concerned that he had placed me in jeopardy. I told him we were surrounded and protected by people who cared about us, and nothing would break that shell unless he chose to return to his mother. He stuck to his word about living with his sisters, and we passed the days with no disturbances from his mother.

On his last day, Shane hung around my dad's printing shop, watching him make some wedding invitations. Scavenging through some piles of poster board, Shane pulled out three gigantic fluorescent pieces and asked Dad for spray paint. Luckily, my dad didn't know Shane's criminal history, because I think he would have had second thoughts about it. Shane went outside with his materials, and half an hour later he showed us his artwork. He had painted "FRESH" and his name in various scripts, and was wearing a radiant smile that stretched from ear to ear. He offered his work to us like a great prize, and, looking down, said quietly, "Thanks."

Shane arrived safely at the reservation, although Marlina was very disturbed about his being shipped back to the reservation. I received a reprimand from Barbara for my insubordination, but she also said she was very proud of me, and had secretly covered for me whenever the director had hinted at disciplinary action.

Marlina, on the other hand, was haunting the shelter, and even tried to get in by pleading that she had been physically abused and needed a place to stay. Normally, the shelter wouldn't refuse any woman who asked for refuge, but, under the circumstances, hers was an unusual request. After a few phone calls to people "in the know," the beat of the tom-tom (what some call the grapevine) was that Marlina wanted to get into the shelter so she could get to me and teach me not to mess with other people's kids. Evidently there were no takers on her hit offer.

That was all we needed to hear; she was refused shelter. The staff was notified not to allow anyone fitting her description to enter the shelter at any time.

Marlina tried her best to penetrate the shelter walls, and even came to the door, buzzing the intercom, begging for a place to stay. A few advocates became sympathetic to her after she pleaded her case for the umpteenth time, and they began to waver. Their doubts vanished when Marlina turned up at the shelter door again, obviously very drunk, demanding that her son be turned over to her and threatening to beat up the advocate if she wasn't let in to the shelter. The police were called, and Marlina left. A message was sent through the tom-tom that if she returned to the shelter she would be arrested.

That seemed to place a damper on Marlina's quest, and after a few failed attempts to catch me when I was arriving or leaving work, she faded into oblivion. Or so I thought. I let my guard down because I couldn't continue to function, living in such intense fear. About a month after Shane left, I was driving to work on a fresh, sunny morning, with the convertible top down on my car and the stereo turned up. I loved the feeling it gave me of being free, wind flowing through my hair, one step removed from the rest of the world. As I drove down a busy one-way street in the Native American neighborhood, a few blocks from the shelter, I felt something whiz by my right check and hit the rear window. Thinking it was a large bug or a stone from a passing truck (my little Fiat X1/9 sat close to the ground), I continued driving. Not until I parked the car did I notice that my rear window looked like a spider's web. It was completely shattered. At the center of the web, which was on the driver's side behind my head, was a bullet hole.

I was frightened that I had narrowly missed a bullet to my head, and it was more than I could comprehend. I was angry that I was innocently driving down a public street and violated by some crazed lunatic. It took me a couple of minutes before I remembered the so-called hit. I called the police, but they didn't place much credence in the hit theory. They stated that drive-by shootings had recently increased in that area of the city. There wasn't anything they could do for me besides filing the report and advised me to change my route to work. To this day I don't know if it was Marlina's hit, but I was very nervous for months after that near miss.

If I sound somewhat detached from the whole experience, it's because, working at a shelter, I had become accustomed to dramas. It was commonplace in my work day to talk to a woman on the crisis line who was contemplating suicide, or drive a woman to her abuser's home to grab her children and get them to the shelter. Then there were bomb threats from upset boyfriends, and children explicitly revealing sexual molestation by their mothers' pimps. So, in retrospect, a bullet through one's window just seemed like another minor happenstance in a typically extraordinary day. Not everyone can handle such turmoil and conflict, but, because of my own dysfunctional background and personal traumas, I seemed to thrive on the day-to-day drama.

My Grandmother had raised me because my mother, a single parent, worked full time. My parents separated when I was four months old and didn't reconcile until after Grandma's death. I was seven years old. Funny, I had this vivid illusion that my faceless father looked like Dean Martin the movie star, during his better years, and I was shocked when I met him for the first time in my whole life. He didn't look at all like any movie star, just an ordinary guy, who had the nerve to kiss my mother. And in front of me.

I supect the timing on this reunification wasn't coincidental. Grandma hated the thought of her only daughter marrying a 'dirty

Mexican' (her terminology); in those days, the mid 1950's it was considered even more horrendous than marrying a Black man. Remember the classic interracial movie, *To Sir With Love*?

Their marriage could not endure Grandma's wrathfulness, even after her death. They separated and reunited numerous times, with a lingering taste of bitterness on their tongues, and eventually divorced when I was 13 years old.

A full-blooded German, Grandma was a strong, determined woman. According to my mother, grandma had 'powers'. My mother warned me that Grandma saw through closed doors and predicted the future. Sometimes I entertained the thoughts that mom was slightly exaggerating Grandma's skills, nonetheless, I did fear her. These powers were never fully explained to me, although I asked my mother often. I remember sitting in Grandma's lap staring into her deep blue eyes and listening to stories about her life.

Our bond deepened after her death, and for many years I didn't believe she had actually died because she visited me every night in my dreams. Grandmother was a very destructive person though, instilling such tremendous fear in my mother, that she remains terrified of her to this day. For reasons that are purely conjecture, Grandmother chose to rule my mother from her grave through a very vindictive inheritance. She passed over her own daughter and gave the bulk of her estate to me, her granddaughter. This caused alienation between myself and my mother, which I speculate was my Grandmother's intention.

3

The "Res"

October

IT WAS A LONG AND BORING DRIVE TO NORTH DAKOTA, THROUGH the inner recesses of the Midwest. The brilliant, sparkling blues and greens of the lakes and trees of Minnesota came to an abrupt end, and the golden wheat hues followed the subtle butte terrain. The buttes are small compared to the giant sweeping slopes surrounding Minot, North Dakota. If I had never seen a mountain range, the buttes would have been impressive, but they just didn't evoke the sense of awe or have the grandeur of the mountains.

As I stared out the window while my co-worker Krissy drove, I wondered how the reservation would differ from the other small towns we were passing through. I had been warned by well-meaning friends not to drive on the reservation at night because the Indians drove their cars without the headlights on. No one could really say why this strange practice was common on reservations, but our informants were quite adamant that Krissy and I avoided driving at night at all costs.

Chuckling to myself, I just couldn't envision an entire population driving at night with no lights on—it didn't make sense. On the other hand, a seed of paranoia had been planted, so I didn't intend to drive at night, in case it was true. I had received other warnings; "single white women weren't allowed on the reservation without an escort". That one I totally ignored; anyway, we'd be with Shane.

"White women were scalped if caught with one of their children."

How long ago did the last scalping incident take place? Come on, give me a break! And then there was an old standby scare tactic—"White women were raped and left for dead and no one ever found their bodies."

I think that covers the wonderful advice we were given. Thank God I was a rebellious individual, because I had received enough "Stop, Do Not Pass Go" cards to discourage the average person.

Anyway, Shane had invited us to visit him, and I wasn't going to disappoint him. Deep down I felt honored that he wanted us to come. While I was hiding him he described the unique aspects of his reservation and Wanagi[1] Lake. Wanagi was the Sioux name for Spirit. He had described the Aspen trees (which Minnesota doesn't have) and how their silvery glow illuminates the way to the reservation. He chattered on about his fishing adventures on the lake and how the wanagi's made people disappear.

Wanagi Lake was an unusual name, and Shane said that, according to his aunt, some preachers had given it the name because the lake had swallowed up a couple of priests. The preachers thought Satan himself inhabited the lake. Shane's people had another name for the lake that wasn't connected with evil. It described the abundance of fish the lake gave to the tribe; but Shane couldn't remember the name because it was Sioux.

We passed one of the many military bases in North Dakota, with fighter planes planted like warts on the runway. I had never seen a war plane before, and the sight left me feeling angry and frustrated. I had always known there were silos planted with rockets and bombs; when I was little, my dad would take us on a Sunday drive, pointing out the silos standing statuesque in the countryside. They looked like regular silos to me, but he swore they stored bombs, so I believed him.

Funny, I didn't remember that childhood memory until I looked at those bombers, and suddenly the dichotomy seemed so strange. Here I was striving to teach adults to be nonviolet to each other and their children while my country continued to fight wars and kill thousands. A momentary flash of realization swept over me. Maybe I couldn't save the world, perhaps I'm being too idealistic about this. I ignored the thought.

'Welcome to Wanagi Lake' beckoned the sign, although it had definitely seen better days, or even better years. The town offered a drive-in liquor store, a highway restaurant, and a motel advertising color television. A right at the traffic light led to main street USA and the route to the dreaded Wanagi Lake.

Stopping for gas, we decided to head into the reservation and pick up Shane before dinner. The gas station attendant, curious to know why city girls were visiting his fair town, asked where we were heading. When we told him our destination, he became silent.

He frowned and his voice dropped a few octaves, "I don't think you girls should go there. Injuns live there, ya know."

We thanked him for his concern, and told him we were visiting a relative. He gave us the once-over (we didn't resemble Sioux by any stretch of the imagination), shrugged, and walked away. It was obvious that the people of Wanagi Lake and the surrounding area didn't advertise their neighboring reservation in any of its tourist brochures.

The lake itself bordered the reservation and flanked both sides of the highway. I had a sense of foreboding as I saw the pale grays of the late afternoon being reflected in the water. I watched the whitecaps rippling over its dull surface. It wasn't the kind of lake that I'd sit by in a beach chair and gaze into its depths. This lake appeared to demand respect and reflected the anger and deep resentment felt by its community.

We turned left off the highway and followed the road to the Bureau of Indian Affairs office, where we were required to stop and register. They gave us vague directions to the interim home where Shane was staying.

The tribe had been unable to place him in the same foster home as his sisters, so he'd been thrown into the interim home until a foster home could be found. This wasn't the first time Shane had lived at the interim home: in fact he had been there twice before and hated it with a passion. A few weeks after moving to the reservation, he had called and explained his predicament. I contacted the Tribal Council to see if I could assist with Shane's placement. Even though he had been promised he could live with his sisters, I was told that he was put in the interim home so they could monitor his behavior. I was also reminded that the tribe had custody over him—meaning that I could suggest, but not request.

After two months of phone calls from Shane, his invitation to visit sounded like a plea for help. He hinted many times that he was thinking about running away, but agreed to stay after I promised him to visit. After we left, I knew he'd entertain the notion again.

We crossed two cattle guards, then followed the winding, dusty dirt road until a small tract house came into view. It sat in a valley surrounded by trees. Cows grazed in the pasture to the left of the house, and mangy dogs wandered around the dirt parking area. Feeling as if a thousand eyes were boring into us, Krissy and I stepped out of the car and walked up the path towards the door.

As I started to knock, a man opened the door and ushered us inside. A pool table sat to the right of the doorway; the rest of the room contained couches and a blaring television. About ten adolescent boys were hanging around, trying to stare at us without being too obvious. The man introduced himself as Bryce, one of the day counselors, and chased them away, leading us down a long green hallway into an office. The walls looked as if they had been punched in various places, but, on the whole, the building was in reasonable condition. I certainly wouldn't want to live there, though: it had a suffocating, institutional air about it.

After small talk about our long drive, Bryce got down to the nitty-gritty. Shane was not doing as well as anticipated, and the interim home staff were hoping that we could shed some light on his poor behavior. Keeping my temper as best I could, I explained that Shane had been made a promise about being able to live with his sisters. I said that I wasn't surprised at his declining cooperation because he must be frustrated and disappointed about having been misled. Shane was being undermined by the tribe for reasons I couldn't begin to fathom. I also felt somewhat defensive, wondering if I was somehow to blame for supporting Shane's decision to return here. I must have appeared somewhat angry because the counselor quickly became apologetic and suggested that Shane might benefit from individual counseling.

Just then the door burst open and Shane ran into the room, a brilliant smile lighting up his face. Laughing, we all hugged and began talking all at once as Shane led us to his room. He wanted to get out of the interim home as quickly as possible, so he grabbed a jacket, and we piled into the car and headed into town for dinner.

After eating, we drove to Allana and Missy's house in the dark. I told Shane the warnings we had heard about the reservation, and he giggled helplessly at what he called an old wives' tale. We pulled into a circular drive with tract homes lined up like bowling pins. Shane ran up to one of the doors, yelling for his sisters. We followed closely as the neighbors began to open their doors and stare at us. Kids bolted out of houses, making a beeline for the car. As I entered the foster mother's house, I glanced back and saw them stroking the finish and staring in through the windows. There must have been thirteen kids surrounding the car.

Cammie, the foster mother, was a kind, sweet woman, who made us feel completely at home. The girls were really excited to see us, bringing out their new clothes. Shane ran outside when we sat down to have coffee, but he returned a few minutes later, yelling, "There's a ton of kids jumping up and down on your car. Gimme the keys, and me and my sisters will sit inside; then the kids will go away."

I looked at Shane, wondering if he was planning on driving to Minnesota that night, but decided I had to trust him and handed over the keys.

As he and his sisters went out to the car, I got up and drew the curtain back from the window. Twenty or more kids were now swarming around the car like bees in a honeycomb, and Shane was pushing them away from the passenger's side so he and his sisters could get in. We had rented a car because Krissy and I both had two-seater cars, so I was relieved to see the kids fall back as Shane climbed in. He then proceeded to crank the radio so loud that we could hear it clearly in the house. As Krissy and Cammie talked, I thought of all the warnings people had given me, and realized how fearful people are of the unknown.

While giving us the grand tour of the reservation, Shane recounted his trips to the bar in town with his mother while he was growing up. He would wait in the car, sleeping, until Marlina had finished imbibing; then he would jump in the driver's seat and chauffeur her home—at age six! Questioning how he could reach the foot pedals, he rolled his eyes and said he used the shifter and jammed it into 'drive' and 'park'. He considered those days as happy times because at least he was able to be with his mother and help her out. It was very hard for me to relate to them as good times.

Shane took us to the local candy store, which was actually a house whose occupants sold candy and sodas on the porch, and showed us the abandoned fort. It was in perfect condition, as if the military were still in residence. Desks and chairs sat ready to greet the officers, and the mess hall looked ready to serve food.

The fort was established in 1870. It's intention was to place two different bands of Sioux tribes on a designated piece of land and build a post to protect the overland route extending from southern Minnesota to western Montana. The harsh winters resulted in various Sioux tribes, alienated from their own lands, to seek shelter at the fort. Eventually the officer in command allotted food rations to prevent the Indians from dying. Within ten years, the Indians were relocated on individual portions of land. The fort had a surrealistic atmosphere, and I felt very uncomfortable being there.

Leading us down a sloping hill at the rear, Shane pointed to a cave. "That," he said, "is where the Indians would hide out so they wouldn't get caught, and that's where I go when I have to get away from everything."

I looked into the cave cut into the hill. An image flashed before me of all the people who had hidden there, hoping the earth would give them the shelter they were unable to find anywhere else. "So, is this where you'll go after we leave?" I hinted.

Shane ignored me and walked away, heading for the car. I decided to drop the issue; for the time being.

We drove past the various houses where Shane had stayed when his mother had left him, and he told us why he was so afraid of the dark. When he was about four years old, a foster family used to lock him in the closet while they went into town, sometimes leaving him in there for the entire day. He finally ran away, only to be caught and returned to the same family.

As we drove by another house in the countryside, he divulged his memory of the foster mother who had poured Tabasco down his throat whenever he wouldn't answer her. It was hard to imagine how someone could do that to such a sweet child. Shane had a happy-go-lucky air about him that drew people towards him, and a smile that could cheer a depressed person. What a tragedy that he had to experience such pain.

Shane saved the best for our last day: the Hutopah[2] National Forest, where free-roaming buffalo lumbered through the plains. It was a drive-through preserve, one of those "don't feed the animals or get out of your car for any reason" places; although all the kids hiked the buffalo trails, disregarding the warnings. Herds of buffalo crossed the road, acting as if the car was an ant in their path. They looked thick and woolly, wearing their heavy coats for the harsh winter ahead. We took our time, enjoying the trees in their fall reds, golds, and browns.

In a secluded grove of trees on the edge of the national forest, we stopped to bury ourselves in the huge piles of leaves. When Missy didn't want to come out from under her blanket of leaves, Allana and I left her for a while and walked along a small dirt road. This was our first time alone, and it was obvious that something was bothering her. Without hesitation, Allana told me she had tried to commit suicide a few weeks earlier. It caught me so off guard I didn't know what to say. I had thought she was happy; her foster mother seemed nurturing and supportive. I asked her why, and all she could say was that she missed her real mother. She had heard that her mother wanted to see her, but the tribe wouldn't allow Marlina on the reservation until she met with the Tribal Council. I empathized with Allana, she felt mixed up and confused, but I didn't know how to help her. I looked up at the sky and asked silently, 'Why, God? Why do these children have to go through so much pain at such an early age?'

I answered Allana as best I could, telling her that she didn't need to die; there were people who loved and cared about her. Then I suggested she go to a counselor. Luckily, she had already started going, but said that it wasn't the same as talking to me. I assured her that she could call me anytime, day or night, and if she lost my phone number she could ask Shane for it. That was all I could do, I had enough trying to maintain control with Shane. I felt too young and inexperienced to be dealing with suicidal children. I handled Allana's dilemma with one of my most utilized coping skills; put it away, in the back of my mind for another day, sort of a Scarlet O'Hara mentality.

By our third day on the reservation, the entire population seemed to know us. Strangers greeted us by name as we walked around, saying "You're the girls visiting Shane, aren't you?"

We had only one day left, and I felt sorry to be leaving. On the surface I saw horrendous poverty, and a sense of apathy; but on a deeper level, there was a comforting presence, like a snuggly down comforter. The land vibrated with a resonance. The closeness these people historically had with their land emitted tranquility, this land was deeply loved and respected. I didn't want to leave.

We ended our stay with a rousing game of bingo at the local church, and, after quickly saying good-bye to everyone, drove back into the white man's world.

4

New Beginnings

January

MY CONTACT WITH SHANE WAS SOMEWHAT SPORADIC FOR THE next few months. I called him every few weeks, and occasionally he would call me. I was very aware of the fact that keeping his friends in the Twin Cities would continue to pull him back here and remind him of his mother. I always felt I walked a fine line with him—not drawing him too close for fear of confusing him, yet I wanted him to know I would always be there for him if he needed me. This tug of war pulled on my heart, but I wanted what was best for Shane, even if it meant distancing myself from him.

I dealt with my conflicting feelings by playing 'Superwoman'. I held a full-time administrative/psychotherapy job at a domestic abuse agency, attended graduate school full time, and juggled a new relationship.

Needless to say, not all my decisions were the most appropriate ones, and ranking high on that list was my relationship with Hassad, a student from Libya. We met at a nightclub in Minneapolis. I was out with friends from work playing my bar game. I never had difficulty finding men to ask me to dance, but I needed a filter to screen out the jerks. When Hassad asked me to dance, I willingly accepted.

He was the classic tall, dark, and handsome, and very charismatic, with an intriguing accent. As we danced, the inevitable question came up: "Where do you work?"

Smiling shyly, I answered, "In a battered women's shelter."

There was usually one of two reactions by men to my occupation. In one, the guy would drop my hand, stare at me, and exclaim defensively, "I never hit women. I never hit my girlfriends."

Too defensive, probably an abuser, I'd think. In the other, he'd say something like, "Oh, you're one of those women's libbers. I suppose you'll call me a male chauvinistic pig, right?"

In both cases I thanked the guy and avoided him for the remainder of the evening. When I played my game with Hassad, he smiled, looked into my eyes, and said, "Oh, really. Sounds interesting."

He passed! We spent the rest of the evening together, and then went back to his apartment. I thought I'd never see him again. I wasn't interested in a relationship; my life was too full. Just out of curiosity, I left my business card on his pillow, thanking him and wishing him luck. Was I worried about AIDS or sexually transmitted diseases? I'm embarrassed to say I wasn't. This was the sexual revolution, and I was enjoying it. Can't say I'd do it again in this day and age, but I was one of the lucky ones who didn't get caught.

Hassad called me the next day, and I felt pleased but was quite cool towards him. We arranged to go out together the following weekend. He sent flowers and courted me as if I were his princess. Well, before long, I fell head over heels for Hassad. As he sensed that he was winning me over, he began to distance himself, and we played with each other's emotions, distancing and pursuing pursuing and distancing, otherwise known as the 'fear of intimacy' game. Love won out and, two months later, he proposed to me. Slipping the ring on my finger, he explained that he had almost backed out because he feared I was too beautiful and sophisticated for him. Try saying no to that!

We eloped to South Dakota the following week. Hassad chose South Dakota because their marriage policy excluded a five day waiting period. Sensing my reluctance over the urgency, he promised that we would have a formal wedding in the summer.

Friends and family were shocked. This impulsiveness was so out of character for me that they were very worried. After a few of my girlfriends had met him, they certainly understood how he had hooked me, but that increased rather than alleviated their concern for me. Oh, and by the way, this was the time that Colonel Qhadafi was threatening to blow up the United States with the aid of terrorists. Any man who looked Arabic, and especially one who was actually Libyan, was discriminated against, and sometimes beaten up. At a popular nightclub Hassad and I frequented, our table was surrounded by young macho rednecks threatening to beat him up. I was also called, among other obscenities, a traitor to my country. Yes, my friends had reason to be worried about me.

To be honest, I had some reservations, but whenever my intuition whispered to me, I ignored it and willed it away. The only time my intuition really screamed at me was on my wedding day. We were waiting for the judge to arrive, he was an hour late; I looked at the door, looked at Hassad and, with all my will, suppressed an urge to bolt out the door before it was too late. I convinced myself that too much money had been spent on a dress . . . I'd let my friends down . . . so I couldn't change my mind. And I didn't. But within twelve hours I knew I had made a terrible mistake.

As we were driving back from South Dakota, I was staring out the window at the blur of trees lining the road. My mind was blank, and Hassad was driving in silence. My thoughts went to my parents and how they had married. My grandmother was adamantly opposed to the marriage so my parents had eloped while she was hospitalized for a nervous breakdown. I remembered seeing their wedding pictures, with only a few people attending the ceremony. Our wedding had the judge's wife and daughter were our only attendees... My God, I'm doing exactly the same thing as my mother did. She married a Mexican, which in those days was socially unacceptable, creating a scandal in her family. To top it off, she also divorced him. I was eloping with a Libyan, which was also socially unacceptable. A sick feeling of dread grew in my stomach—I was repeating my parent's history.

The marriage lasted for three weeks. I caught Hassad cheating on me and kicked him out of my condo. He tried to justify his behavior with various excuses, but I had known the marriage was finished the day it began. I suggested marriage counseling, but he wouldn't hear of it, maintaining his innocence until the day of the divorce. Our cultures were at polar opposites, and we were caught in the middle, unable to separate our emotions from the clashing of the two worlds. When I tried to explain this marriage to others, I would sum it up in a saying of my own making: "Never marry a one-night stand."

That was undervaluing what I had learned. My relationship with Hassad forced me to address deep parent–child relationship issues. I put myself into therapy for a year. I wished this lesson could have been less painful, but I did learn.

May

Shane's timing couldn't have been worse. Besides juggling school and work, I was in therapy and filing for divorce when his phone call came. It was early on a Saturday evening, and I was at my computer, absorbed in writing a term paper. We had talked a week earlier, so he caught me off guard.

"Guess what?" he exclaimed. "Me and my counselor think it's a good idea for me to live with you."

Agh! It was finally happening. Shane was reaching out to me, trusting me, and I was going through a major life change. I didn't want him to feel rejected, so we talked for a while, and I promised I'd investigate foster care requirements that Monday. But I knew I couldn't qualify to be a foster parent because I had a one-bedroom condo and, because of his age, Shane had to have a separate bedroom.

I called Shane's counselor Bryce, the following day, curious to know how this decision had been reached without my knowledge. Bryce explained that plans for Shane's foster placement had fallen through. It was to have been with a family on the reservation that Shane had stayed with as a child, and Shane had been looking forward to living there again. For reasons the counselor didn't elaborate on, the tribe had suddenly decided the woman didn't measure up to their social services standards, even though this placement had been under consideration for over a year. I explained that I didn't qualify as a foster parent, and Bryce was disappointed, telling me that Shane thought the world of me. That made me feel even more guilty, and I promised him that I would find a safe, nurturing home for Shane.

I called friends who knew Shane, but they weren't able to help me or take him. Then I thought of Krissy. I called her and proposed a plan: I would take Shane for weekends and holidays if she could take him during the week and be the official foster parent. She had an extra bedroom and a full-time job, so she could probably qualify. This way, I would be able to work on my degree on week nights, and Krissy would have her weekends free. After checking with her roommate, Krissy applied to be a foster parent and was accepted, specifically for Shane Lone Eagle.

It's very unusual for a white, single woman to be a foster parent for a Native American. The Indian Child Welfare Act of 1978[1] had stringent restrictions on who could foster Native Americans. Relatives were given priority for foster age; next on the list were Native American families, followed by Native American friends. Non-Indian families were at the bottom of the list. This was to ensure that children were placed within their own culture as much as possible. Krissy didn't run into difficulties because all possibilities had been exhausted for Shane: no one wanted him. It was virtually unheard of for someone in Krissy's situation to be awarded this type of foster care. This illustrated Shane's desirability in terms of foster placement.

After explaining the situation with Shane, I asked him to think about how he would handle living in a lesbian household. He had already known that Krissy was a lesbian, she was open about her sexual preference, but I assured him that if he felt uncomfortable with her sexuality we would think of another arrangement. Shane was disappointed, he had a hard time understanding why I couldn't take him full time, but when I explained that he needed his own bedroom at his age, he agreed. I again asked him to think about living with Krissy and decided to broach the subject in the near future.

We kept the details of our plan secret because social services would never have agreed to such an arrangement. I told Bryce that Krissy had offered to take Shane and she was qualified as a foster parent.

Bryce was surprised and said that if Shane was comfortable with that decision, he'd go along with it. By this time Shane was enthusiastic, and the placement process began. Krissy lived in a three-bedroom duplex in Powderhorn Park. Shane was ecstatic at the thought of having his own private bedroom. "I'll get a stereo, a black light, and posters on the wall. No girlie posters, though—I know you guys don't like that stuff." Oh that Shane. Always saying what people wanted to hear.

I was nervous and excited that Shane had reached out to me. I was also scared because I was assuming responsibility for another person's life, and my decisions would radically affect him. No more impulsive whims; I had a child to think about, and that child would not be easy to take care of. Shane had been institutionalized for most of his life, and family life, although he'd longed for it, was foreign to him. I was taking on a thirteen year old—only twelve years younger than myself.

The only remaining obstacle was the Tribal Court hearing, which legalized the placement and allowed family members to protest against it. The Tribal Court also had the power to negate the interim home's placement recommendation.

Shane was very apprehensive about the hearing, calling me nightly for support and reassurance. He controlled his impulse to run away until he heard rumors that his mother would be at the hearing to protest placement and demand custody of him. I worried that Shane might feel pressured to stay with Krissy and me, and perhaps secretly wished that he could go with his mother.

I talked with Shane at length, reassuring him that he could live with his mother if he chose to, that he wouldn't disappoint me or Krissy. His reaction surprised me. He was adamantly opposed to living with his mother and threatened to run away if the Tribal Court granted her custody. I tried to quiet his fears, but as the hearing day approached, he worked himself into a frenzy. The interim home director, Laura, contacted me and suggested I come and visit Shane to alleviate his fears. I left for the reservation the weekend before the hearing.

I was on the night train heading towards North Dakota, and I couldn't sleep. My mind reeled with thoughts of how my life changed when Shane entered it. Staring into the blackness outside my window,

I was flooded with memories of the first time Shane had stayed at the shelter— risking my job to hide him, and my first visit to the reservation. If only I could see as far into the future as I could see into the past, perhaps then I could get an idea of where I was heading. What role was Shane going to play in my life?

The hours ticked by slowly as I traversed the heartland of the Midwest. I saw flickers of light and imagined families sleeping in their warm, cozy homes. I wondered how many children were crying themselves to sleep in fear of being abused; how many women were praying that this would be the last day of violence from their husbands? Then I told myself I was looking at life through jaded eyes. I'd been involved with domestic abuse for too long and saw it everywhere. I sighed and wondered if there were any happy families left.

I drifted off to sleep but awoke abruptly, remembering why I was on the train. I couldn't control Shane's actions, even though I tried, but I hoped his emotions would settle down once I was there. The effects would be devastating if he ran away before the hearing. I had to convince Shane that running away would be perceived negatively by the Tribal Council. That wouldn't be easy because adolescents have difficulty seeing that, although adults may understand someone's motives, they don't necessarily condone the actions. I felt so green, so inexperienced at all of this. Here I was being plummeted into motherhood to tackle adolescence, without having had the experience of birthing or dealing with childhood.

Half an hour from now the sun would rise above the stark, barren prairie, but, as I walked outside, cold, crisp air assaulted me. I glanced up and down the street and saw a single car approaching the station. Apart from that, the town of Wanagi Lake was still. I always experienced culture shock when I visited the area. The pace was much slower here, and I seemed to be two steps ahead of everything for the first few hours.

The navy blue Ford pulled up in front of me, and a blonde woman in her thirties leaned across the seat and opened the passenger door. I tossed my bag into the back seat and jumped in. "Hi, I'm Laura, the interim home director. We met before, on your last visit, remember?"

To be honest, I didn't. I had seen so many new faces during that time, but I didn't want to insult her, so I nodded. We exchanged pleasantries about my trip on the way to her house.

Once there, she packed her son off to school and, explaining that Shane would be at school until about three-thirty, asked if I wanted to sleep and shower at her home. I gratefully accepted her offer because my hotel room wouldn't be ready till two o'clock, and I was exhausted.

Late in the afternoon Laura dropped me off at the interim home with a few friendly warnings. Head lice was common among the kids and, although Shane didn't have them yet, the boys were into wearing each other's hats. Ironically, one of the first things Shane did when he saw me was toss the hat he was wearing onto my head. Also, the kids were hyperactive because of Shane's impending hearing, and Shane had been talking to them about running away. I certainly had my job cut out for me.

Shane was sitting in a small office getting his photo taken for a contest. His face lit up when I walked in, but he didn't want to seem too eager—he had to maintain his cool. We exchanged greetings, and I waited for him to finish. Transitions (beginnings and endings) were always difficult for Shane. This was common for children who have been abused; they don't know how to handle their emotions, so they shut down. During a fleeting moment of trust, Shane had shown me his lower lip, which had a white scar near the left corner. He described how his mother had thrown a shoe at him in a fit of rage, and the heel had caught his lower lip. I knew this was one of an infinite list of abuses he endured.

Because Shane had experienced such abrupt and tragic events in his life, he had built up defenses to buffer the hurt. Typically, he'd withdraw physically and emotionally into himself, communicating in monosyllables and avoiding eye contact. Needless to say, people's arrivals and departures were very uncomfortable times for him. Even though I knew this intellectually, it didn't make it any easier. And sometimes I forgot and took his behavior personally. This visit was no exception.

We played checkers and ate dinner with the rest of the residents. I avoided talking about the hearing because Shane seemed on edge. We would have plenty of time to talk later. I was watching television with some of the kids when Shane announced that he had a session with his psychiatrist. "Do you want to come?" he asked.

I was tired and didn't really want to meet his psychiatrist tonight, but I could tell by his face that it was important to him. I followed him to a storage room—the counseling room. Bryce waited with us, and we chatted until the psychiatrist arrived. Shane was quiet and withdrawn, attempting to blend with the concrete wall behind him.

With a flurry, the door flew open and a young, attractive, olive-skinned man in his late thirties swept into the room. He gave the impression of being disorganized. His clothes were in disarray, and papers were sticking out of his worn leather briefcase. Adelson introduced himself to me, saying that he was a graduate intern from Minot, North Dakota. "Shane tells me you work with children," he stated.

"Yes, I'm working at a domestic abuse therapy agency as a children's therapist and assistant director, and I also worked with abused children at a battered women's shelter for three years." For some reason, I felt as if I was in the hot seat.

"Hmm," Adelson replied, "and Shane is going to live with you, right?"

I explained that Shane would be living with Krissy, who qualified for foster care licensing, but that I would have constant contact with Shane. Now I knew what it was like to be on the receiving end of a parent-child therapy session. I also reaffirmed my vow never to be late for a session—it left the impression of unprofessionalism.

"Shane," Adelson yelled, turning to look at him.

Shane started out of his chair, wearing a spaced-out expression, and responded, "Yeah."

"What do you think about living in Minneapolis?"

Shane rocked back on his chair, balancing it on two legs, with a blank stare. "It's fine."

Adelson reached over, steadied Shane's chair and said, "Come on now, you know the rules."

Shane whistled part of a rap song, rocked back and forth on the chair, sighed, and said, "Okay, I want to live there." He looked into my eyes and enunciated, "I want a family, and she's it."

My heart filled with joy, but a question that I had been harboring for a while surfaced, and I asked, "Are you going to miss living on the reservation and being with your people?"

Shane looked first at me, then at Adelson. He paused and, making direct eye contact with both of us, replied, "I'm Indian on the reservation and off. I don't forget who I am; it's in my blood. Just because I'm not living with Indians doesn't mean I'm not one. I'm Indian now and forever."

The room was silent. It was obvious that he had given this subject much thought, and I was surprised at the deep wisdom that he displayed. The session wound down, with Adelson and Bryce thanking me for spending time with Shane before the hearing. I was so proud of Shane. He had so much potential; he just needed someone to care enough to tap the source. I wanted to be that person.

The next day brought a blanket of fresh snow, which melted within a few hours. Shane and I decided to walk to his sisters' foster home, about two miles away. We took our time, enjoying the warm sunlight and northern breeze. I decided this was a good time to have a heart-to-heart talk with Shane about Krissy. I had rehearsed bringing up the subject. Since he would be living with Krissy, I needed to know if he could handle her sexual preference. I asked Shane how he thought it would be living with Krissy. "Great, no problem."

"And what about her being a lesbian?"

He laughed and said, "I know she's a lesbian."

"I know it doesn't bother you, but what about your friends? When they come over, they might see something that embarrasses them."

With anger in his eyes, he stared at me and said, "If they don't like it, they don't have to come over.".

I explained that sometimes people don't like gays or lesbians. He agreed, saying that kids say gross stuff about them. I asked him why they did that. "Cause they're dumb!"

I replied that a lot of people are afraid of other people's lifestyles. They think that if they learn to understand and accept homosexuals, they might catch it and become gay themselves. Shane agreed, but his eyes were following a teenage girl riding a bike down the road. I had lost his attention, but at least I knew he was aware of other people's perceptions.

We arrived at Allana and Missy's house and sat talking for a while. Both girls asked if they could come and live with me. Allana told me they hated it at their foster home and insisted on knowing why Shane was the lucky one who could live with me. I tried to explain that Shane hadn't been so lucky—he'd lived in the interim home for a year and hated it. Missy forced the issue, and I told her that Krissy and I just didn't have enough room, not to mention time and energy, for all of them. Much as I would like to see the family reunited, this just wasn't the right time. "Humph, Shane always gets the best, and we get nothing," Missy lamented.

I wasn't worried about the girls; they were in a stable, healthy environment and would get over their resentment. We said goodbye to the girls and, on our walk back, I asked Shane if the girls had ever mentioned wanting to live with Krissy and me. They hadn't, so I explained that his sisters felt left out. He was quiet for a while, then said softly, "It'd be nice if we'd live together; it's been so long since we have." I expressed to him that maybe it would happen some day, but first we had to get him settled.

We spent hours hiking through the Hutopah National Forest, amongst the buffalo. After my initial apprehension, I began to enjoy the buffalo, and Shane treated them like large dogs. We continued our checkers championship, and I taught Shane to play backgammon. He quickly learned the moves and became a worthy opponent. His analytical, detail-oriented mind flourished when he played games and pool.

The boys at the interim home took an interest in me and, after a day or two, I became their sounding board, listening to the trials and tribulations of their daily life. I wanted to take them all to a safe home where they could enjoy being part of a family. Their ages ranged from ten to seventeen, and most of them had lived at the home for a large part of their lives. A few boys had tried going back to live with their families but, because of continued alcohol and physical abuse, had been returned to the interim home.

One teenager was an example of a walking time bomb. If one small thing went wrong, he'd explode. I was careful around him and tried not to get in his way. During my four-day stay, two boys ran away, and the police were called. Another boy had a fist fight with a staff member and was put in the adult jail on the reservation. Shane's roommate was sixteen and had a thirty-three year old girlfriend. He talked constantly about females and sex, and liked to hang around me. I asked him if he had been in counseling. He admitted that he'd gone a couple of times but said the counselor had told him stuff he already knew. He insisted that he didn't want to change his behavior—he liked female attention and sex. I knew that he wasn't ready to hear anything I had to say, so I just listened.

The day I was leaving, twelve-year-old twin boys who had lived at the interim home six years out of their young lives, asked if they could also live with me. They didn't know where their mother was, and the rest of their family had disappeared. Both appeared quiet and shy, but were seething under the surface. I explained why I couldn't help them, and they told me they had known I would refuse but thought they would take a chance at it anyway. The desperation and hopelessness I saw in those children's eyes overwhelmed me. So many children are in need of love and attention, yet few people are willing to take the risks involved. If I could help just one child, my life purpose would be fulfilled.

5

Home to Roost

June

I LEFT SHANE THE DAY BEFORE THE HEARING. HE WAS LESS ANXious and had promised not to run away until the Tribal Court had made its decision. Throughout his life adults had made numerous promises to him, which they rarely kept. As a result he didn't have much faith in them.

The Tribal Court was governed by a council consisting of the tribal chairman and council members elected from the reservation's six districts. This council ruled over the 5,000 members of the tribe and 60,000 acres of reservation land.

My heart was heavy as we waited for my train and I hugged Shane. EagleHeart (my teacher, mentor, and friend) and I had discussed the high suicide rate among native American teenagers. At that time, fifty percent of them would attempt suicide. We speculated whether the culture and the Native American race as a whole were being annihilated from within, and at a rapid rate. To me, Shane represented not only all the boys at the reservation's interim home but also all the forgotten children. Without help, nurturing, and intervention, these children would set out to destroy themselves and take their rage out on the world that was so cruel to them.

Krissy arrived at the reservation within twenty-four hours of my departure; she had been petitioned to attend the hearing. She and Shane had promised to call me as soon as they heard the judgment. The hearing started at ten o'clock, and each time the phone rang after that, I prepared myself. After a few false alarms, I tried to relax and focus on my work. Finally, at two o'clock, Shane called. "Hi, Deb," he said casually.

"Well?" I replied.

Shane continued to toy with me and let me guess the result. Ugh, teenagers! He dragged the agony out a little longer until I screamed into the phone, "Shane!"

He laughed and yelled, "I'm coming home!"

His mother hadn't shown up at the hearing, and I think he had mixed emotions about that—another rejection from his mother. Krissy came on the phone and filled me in on the details. The Tribal Court hadn't awarded her full custody because she wasn't Sioux, which meant that the tribe was still the final authority in matters concerning Shane, even though he wouldn't be residing on the reservation. The Tribal Court Magistrate had asked Shane where he wanted to live. After Shane's testimony that his mother drank and hit him, the magistrate had seemed satisfied that Shane didn't want to live with his mother, and he granted foster care to Krissy.

Shane took the night train, arriving at six o'clock the following Sunday morning. Krissy and I were so excited that we arrived at the station over a half hour early. The train's arrival was announced, and people trickled out of the compartments. We watched about thirty people coming through the turnstile, but no Shane. Finally, he hopped off the train, a small duffel bag slung over his shoulder. He stood there for a while rubbing his eyes, then lumbered up the platform, looking around for familiar faces. After we had exchanged hugs, Shane told us how the little kids sitting next to him had kept him awake for the entire journey. He was exhausted.

Krissy told him we wanted to go out for breakfast, and he agreed, complaining about how expensive the food had been on the train. I picked up Shane's small bag and asked him if he had checked his other luggage. That was all he had—the kids at the interim home had stolen most of his clothes after they found out he was leaving. Krissy and I looked at each other and nodded; we'd have to take him shopping — soon.

Shane's first week in his new life was wonderful. We shopped for shirts, underwear, socks, and shoes. He had been allotted two pairs of socks and underwear a month in the interim home. If his clothes were stolen (which they frequently were), he wasn't able to replace them until the following month.

Like all teens, Shane had expensive tastes and wanted to wear designer clothes. He set his heart on some expensive Reeboks and tried to convince me that they were a great deal. Every time we passed a shoe store he'd look at me with sad puppy eyes and begged, "Please, can I have those Reeboks?".

We had already used up his clothing allowance, and my budget couldn't accommodate those shoes. That didn't dissuade Shane, he called shoe stores to compare prices and look for the best deal. I argued that we could use the money to buy two pairs of shoes. I then tried changing the subject, hoping he'd forget about the shoes. Shane, on the other hand, relentless in his quest for Reeboks, cut ads out of magazines and pasted them on the refrigerator and the bathroom mirror. Since his fourteenth birthday was a week away, Krissy and I split the cost of the shoes and gave them to him as a birthday present. He was in seventh heaven.

Krissy went through her share of power struggles with Shane over which school he should attend. We both wanted him to go to the Native American school in St. Paul, which was small and offered a good student-to-teacher ratio, but Shane would have none of it. He wanted to go to a large school that had computers, basketball courts, and a swimming pool. After exploring and discussing his options (actually we explored, Shane ignored), Shane ended up attending a public school in Krissy's neighborhood, which had a rough reputation. It was also in his mother's old neighborhood. He was happy—we were nervous.

At the end of his second week, we had our first family meeting. Krissy and I talked about house rules, the consequences if he broke them, and dating and drinking. We didn't get very far. As we talked,

Shane stared into space. After about fifteen minutes, Shane reluctantly agreed to the rules, and the meeting ended. Krissy and I reassured each other that he needed more time to adjust, and, next time, we wouldn't let him get away without participating.

We celebrated Shane's fifteenth birthday with all his friends from the shelter. Shane was so happy opening his presents; cracking jokes and hugging everyone in sight, he floated on clouds that whole day. This was the first birthday party he had been given since he was four years old, and we made it a special day for him. I was so thrilled to see him enjoying himself and others. He went around hugging everyone and saying how lucky he was that people cared about him so much. This was the first time I could remember seeing him truly happy.

Shane had been given a gift certificate for clothes, and the next day we went downtown to shop. As this was his very first gift certificate, he wanted to buy something really special. I was thinking along the lines of a shirt and pants for school, but Shane was dreaming of designer jeans, which would cost the entire amount. After three hours of trying on all the hot clothes, he settled on an exorbitantly expensive pair of jeans. I lectured him on the value of money, but he insisted that it was his gift and he should be able to get anything he wanted. I finally relented, and he ran off to the cashier. Negotiating with a teenager was a lot harder than I had imagined.

He wore his new jeans out of the store and for the rest of the day. That evening we had plans to go roller-skating with my friend and colleague, Natalie. When I asked him if he was going to change into his old jeans, he looked at me as if I was crazy and replied, "No way. There'll be girls there, and I don't want to look like a nerd."

I flashed back to when I was a teenager and had been made to wear ugly clothes. . . so, he wore the jeans.

The roller rink was packed with adolescents, all dressed up in their designer clothes. Shane gave me a see-I-told-you-so smirk and skated off in pursuit of an attractive girl doing spins on the rink. After skating for a while, Natalie and I took a break to watch the kids.

A little while later Shane approached me wearing a puzzled expression and explained that someone had pushed him; he had fallen and ripped his jeans. After making sure he wasn't hurt, I commented that he must be upset, having ripped his new jeans like that. He looked shocked and stated flatly, "No, it's only clothes. It's not like I hurt myself or anything," and skated away.

Disconcerted, I sat there for a few minutes thinking about my priorities in life. He was right; the most important thing was that he was uninjured. Yet I had been raised to place value on material possessions and couldn't shake the feeling that Shane should be punished. If I had torn my new jeans as a teenager, my mother would have been furious—shaming me and making threats. But I certainly didn't want to force Shane to adopt my beliefs. I wanted to guide him into adulthood with nurturing and respect. Shane taught me a difficult but valuable lesson that night.

My life now consisted of studying until the wee hours on week nights, working full time, entertaining Shane on the weekends, while squeezing in a few nights of dancing at the local nightclubs. I had also been promoted to assistant director for a domestic abuse agency, which was challenging and demanding. On Friday afternoons, Shane would take the city bus from downtown Minneapolis to the Midway area of St. Paul and walk the five blocks to my office. We'd leave work at about five o'clock, go home, change clothes, and go out for pizza and to the movies. We saw a lot of movies.

Shane didn't know anyone in St. Paul, and his friends didn't want to travel the fifteen miles to visit, so I was his sole companion. He became my shadow, which had its advantages and disadvantages. By the end of the weekend we would be getting on each other's nerves, and I'd be broke. Although I loved having Shane around, I wasn't accustomed to sharing my space with an adolescent.

He slept on the living room couch and stayed up till three or four in the morning, watching television. I let him play around on my computer and talk on the phone for hours on end. We had similar tastes in music—rap and jive—so we could talk about the different groups and play their music at full blast.

I was constantly aware of the small age difference between us, and felt that I could relate to him more easily than older adults could. By Sunday I was ready for him to return to Krissy's, but by the following Tuesday, I'd begin to miss him and start planning the weekend adventures.

Shane had a harder time adjusting to living with me than I did to living with him. He wasn't used to living in a home environment, and I'd catch him tossing my art objects into the air and turning my waterbed into a trampoline. Gashes appeared in the walls where Shane violently rocked chairs into them; he threw glassware into the sink and broke it. I tried to explain that many of my belongings had sentimental value and were important to me, and that I wanted him to respect them. He'd change his behavior for an hour or so and then absentmindedly slip back into the old pattern. When I repeated my request, he would nod, but soon resume his carelessness.

I don't think he did this to antagonize me; he simply didn't understand my attachment to objects. Eventually he learned to respect my property to some degree, but he never fully understood the reasoning behind it. In his culture, possessions were there for everyone to share. They didn't control his life as they did mine; and our cultures clashed loudly in this area.

I encouraged Shane to participate in the meal preparation as much as possible and looked forward to teaching him how to make his favorite, fried chicken. As I heated up the frying pan, oil sizzling, I called Shane over to help me lay the chicken parts in the hot oil. He stood six feet away from me, and refused to come near the stove. Rubbing his arm with his hand, his eyes became shiny and he appeared to be holding back a flood of tears. Thinking he was upset about something I may have said, I questioned him. Shaking his head he ran out of the kitchen. I followed him and, after several agonizing minutes, learned that hot grease had been thrown in his face. He had a strong fear of sizzling frying pans. For reasons unknown, Shane refused to tell me who did this to him. I assumed it was Marlina.

Our honeymoon period lasted a month. As I began to realize that he didn't need my attention twenty-four hours a day, and stopped giving it, he became resentful and stopped helping around the house. After trying unsuccessfully to engage him in several projects, I thought we would tackle painting the dining room.

It was an easy paint job, with little framework. We covered the white carpet with newspapers and set up our supplies. I showed him how to dip the brush into the peach paint and spread it over the wall. I noticed he was wearing his good clothes and suggested he change into something old. "No," he insisted, "I won't spill anything."

Famous last words. Not more than a minute went by before he dropped a spot of paint on his shirt. It was latex paint, so he ran into the bathroom to wash it out. A few minutes later he brushed a freshly painted wall with the side of his jeans. He disappeared and came back wearing only his swimming trunks and socks. "Now I'm ready for anything!" he laughed.

He grabbed his paint brush and ran a few strokes up and down the wall. Stepping back to admire his work he landed one stockinged foot in the paint tray. After he'd stripped off his socks, I assumed he couldn't do any more damage, but, as he reached up to paint, he managed to drop the brush on his head, covering his hair with paint. I couldn't control my feelings any longer and sat on the floor laughing hysterically. Shane didn't think it was funny. Frustrated, he started whining, "What am I doing wrong? I have paint all over me and you don't have any."

Laughingly, I explained that I had painted before and that he would get the hang of it eventually. He stared at me, shrugged his shoulders, and mumbled that he'd try it once more. He was doing fine until he accidentally knocked the paint can over as he stepped sideways. That did it. He went sobbing into the bathroom, peach footprints trailing behind him, screaming, "I quit!"

He emerged a few minutes later and proceeded to space out in front of the television. I finished painting the dining room alone.

Shane had a rough time blending in at his new school, being teased constantly about his name and ethnic origins. He had studied karate on the reservation, so he was able to fight back without getting brutally injured.

One weekend he arrived upset over a fight he had had with Willie, an Afro-American boy, who sat behind him in history class. Willie had been teasing him during class, calling him 'fag' and 'Chief.' After ignoring the taunts for a week, Shane couldn't take it any more, and he told Willie to meet him after school in an empty classroom. When Willie arrived, Shane jumped out from behind the classroom door and gave him a karate chop to the neck. Willie fell to the ground and Shane jumped on top of him, throwing in a few punches. One blow caught Willie in the nose, and blood gushed down his face and over his chest. Shane ran home.

After Willie didn't come to school for a few days, Shane found out that he had been suspended. Apparently a teacher had caught him coming out of the classroom with blood dripping down his face, and had suspended him for fighting. When I asked why Willie didn't say who beat him up, Shane replied that Willie would have been embarrassed to admit that a little pip-squeak like him had got the best of him.

Laughingly, I reminded Shane he was lucky not to have been caught. He snapped an interesting retort: "I never get caught. I'm smart enough to know when to run!" I didn't realize how prophetic those words would become.

6

A Rose By Any Other Name ...

October

IT WAS FOUR-THIRTY ON A FRIDAY AFTERNOON. NATALIE, who previously met Shane an a roller skating activity, Shane, and I had just picked up the last of the three adolescent girls who were to attend the PepFest at Wadena High School with us. Shane was in heaven, with a captive audience of girls competing for his attention.

The girls already knew each other very well from attending Natalie's therapy group for adolescents in abusive families. They had been hand-picked by Natalie for this weekend event because of their families' alcohol and drug problems. Two of them had run away, hoping to shock their parents into quitting drugs, only to return home to the same old situation. The girls had become hardened at a very young age and deeply mistrusted adults. Even though I worked with some of their younger brothers and sisters, I, too, would have to prove my salt with them. No wonder Shane felt so relaxed with these girls—they were his peers, in more ways than one.

The kids chattered throughout the two-hour drive, with the radio going full blast. It was great to see Shane enjoy himself and let his guard down—a little. I promised myself that I would do all I could to help Shane trust adults, and I hoped this weekend would begin to fulfill that promise.

The PepFest wasn't going to be easy. We would be locked inside the high school from Friday evening to Sunday at noon, and no-one—adults included, was allowed to leave. That bothered me. I had always challenged authority, and I wondered what kind of role model I would be if I tried to sneak out. On the other hand, I was relieved that Shane couldn't run, not without causing a scene, anyway. I was always aware that a memory could cloud his thoughts and he'd try to run from it—literally.

Susan, a lead therapist who had been involved with PepFest for a few years, greeted us outside and briefly explained the weekend's structure. Adults would be assigned to a team of adolescents and stay with that team throughout the entire weekend. The classrooms were our sleeping accommodations, and the adults would sleep in the same rooms as the teens. Recreational activities would be sprinkled between large group educational sessions, involving all 150 teens, and small group counseling sessions. The goal was to learn about chemical abuse, train the adolescents to educate and support one another, and show them that there were adults in the world who were willing to help them.

Susan refused to go into the details of the small groups, saying only that none of us would be in the same group, and that I, who was acting as a volunteer therapist, would not be assigned to Shane's group. I was somewhat uncomfortable with the sketchy details, but decided I'd go with the flow because I wanted to be a good role model for Shane.

Once inside the school, Natalie led us to a notice board and told us to look for our names on the lists to see where we had been assigned. I had been allocated a group of five girls, which I would share with Terry, a lead therapist. Lead therapists had experience in running PepFests but were not necessarily experienced counselors or therapists. We split up and sought out our classrooms, where we would be spending most of the weekend.

The desks had been pushed back so we could sit on the floor in a circle. The girls entered the room feeling as apprehensive as I did, glancing around nervously, while some had a look of terror on their faces. They, too, had been separated from their friends and had lost that cushion of camaraderie teens depended upon so much.

The kids from Wadena High had been hand-picked by their teachers according to scholarly ability (a reward for good grades) and specific needs. Each group was composed of "needy" kids and "smart" kids. I quickly tried to spot the smart ones, using preppie dress and language skills as my criteria. Sad to say, I was on target with every teen. I had hoped societal pressures were minimized in a rural community. Even though I currently worked with a range of school-age kids, I had worked extensively with teens while employed at the battered women's shelter. I had learned that peer pressure, search for identity, and the need to fit into a certain group were the main characteristics of teenagers.

Once we had introduced ourselves, we joined the large group in the main hall, where a speaker sketched out the weekend ahead of us. We were to stay with our fellow group members throughout the weekend. This meant eating, sleeping, and group meetings. Needless to say, a lot of teens didn't like this, and much grumbling filtered through the room. I glanced over at Shane. He was staring into space. I feared he might be wondering how the hell I had talked him into this.

We passed each other in the hallway after the meeting, and he seemed jubilant, saying it sounded like a fun weekend, especially the basketball games. He was much more excited than I was; and, I must admit, had been secretly hoping he would want to leave so that I could use him as my excuse.

I tried to sleep that night, but it was very difficult with giggly girls asking permission to go to the bathroom every half-hour. They couldn't wander around the halls by themselves because this was a coed PepFest, so Terry or I had to accompany them. That soon got very tiresome, but I was grateful I wasn't a floor monitor like some of the volunteers, who had to stroll up and down the halls until morning.

Morning came too fast for me, after about four hours of interrupted sleep. By seven o'clock my group was in the bathroom brushing their hair and putting on makeup. The girls were relatively quiet, whispering to each other, but avoiding eye contact with Terry or me. Only as I put in my contact lenses did I attract their interest. They were fascinated by my ability to put my fingers in my eyes. I refrained from seeming too eager to engage them in conversation knowing that they didn't trust me.

Breakfast was horrible. The food was all right, but the silence was thicker than pea soup. I asked the girls casual questions and they answered with 'Uh Huh', or 'No Ma'am.' I was only a few years older then they were, so I was uncomfortable being called ma'am. I supposed it was something to do with being in a rural area.

Terry and I struggled to make small talk, but I sensed that she didn't feel comfortable with me. Later I found out that Natalie had raved about my therapeutic skills to the PepFest committee; and, because Terry thought of herself as 'only a school teacher,' she felt intimidated by me. So we weren't off to a very good start, considering we were supposed to role model good communication skills.

The day did turn out to be very successful. The girls set aside their stone faces and began sharing their fears and life struggles. One girl shared that she had tried to commit suicide the previous weekend and was very depressed. Another (one of the preppies) admitted that she had been judging some of the other girls, but was now realizing that everyone had similar problems with parents, school, and relationships.

The time went by very quickly, with alternating large and small group sessions. We learned about the family dynamics of chemical dependency: each member plays a role—the loner, the clown, the caretaker, the addict. Later, when I asked Shane which role he assumed with his mother and sisters, he immediately answered, "The loner," describing his feeling of always being on the outside looking in. I told him we would try to change that, but, from the way he looked at me, I could tell he didn't believe me.

By Sunday morning my group had become very tight and supportive. I was seeing less and less of Shane, but caught him shooting baskets by himself during a break. Quietly observing him through my therapist's eyes, I saw a lonely boy who wanted to be with his peers (he was slyly glancing over at a group by the bleachers), but didn't think he would fit in. Too soon he saw me standing by the door and ran over to me. I asked him what he thought of the PepFest, and he bragged about all the friends he had met and how much fun he was having. I nodded, even though I knew he was telling me what I wanted to hear. His body language, eyes shifted towards the floor with crossed arms and one foot tapping on the wood floor, clearly stated that he felt the exact opposite. But it wasn't the time or place for me to deal with it; that was his group's job. I had my own group to deal with.

All in all the weekend was terrific. My group was united. Shane relaxed and actually did make a few friends. Upon our arrival I had immediately noticed that he was the only American Indian there and one of two minority students. During one of our breaks Shane brought up the issue, saying a kid had told him he'd never seen an Injun except on television. When I asked Shane how he felt about that, he said, "Okay, I'm used to it," and ran off to shoot baskets.

I was concerned, though, because he didn't usually bring up such hot issues unless something was bothering him. I also knew how small towns handled minorities, and we were in an isolated community. I talked to Natalie about it, and she promised to bring it up at the bi-hourly lead therapists' meeting so that others could be made aware of the issue. Nothing more was said, but I kept my eyes open.

The weekend ended on a powerful, emotional note. The whole group came together, and the large hall buzzed with energy as waves of emotion swept over each group. Many teens were laughing and crying at the same time, knowing that the end was drawing closer. PepFest had succeeded in creating a womb-like environment for the teens to share experiences and support each other, and they knew the real world would soon be calling them back.

We sang the theme song of PepFest, *The Rose*[1], and everyone, teens and adults, were crying by the time we reached the last verse.

> . . . *just remember in the winter,*
> *far beneath the winter snow*
> *lies the seed that, with the sun's love,*
> *in the spring becomes the rose.*
>
> <u>The Rose,</u> by Amanda McBroom

The words really represented what we had experienced with each other that weekend. As I sang, I searched through the sea of faces looking for Shane, and suddenly my eyes locked with his. He was standing with his group, but it was as if we were alone, singing the words to each other. The song ended. Tears streaming down our checks, we ran to each other and hugged. In that powerful moment we dropped our protection and our hearts touched. I knew then that all the tribulations I had suffered with Shane had been worthwhile.

7

State of Confusion

December

SEVERAL MONTHS AFTER SHANE CAME TO STAY, I BEGAN dating again. Concerned that Shane might feel left out, I asked him how he felt about it. To my surprise he seemed excited at the prospect, and got me to agree that he could play on the computer and talk on the phone the whole time I was gone. His attitude was, "Get out of the house so I can have some fun." I felt guilty about leaving him alone and worried that he might get into trouble, but I had to start trusting him.

One night as I was getting ready to go dancing with James, a man I was starting to date, Shane asked me how old you had to be to get into a nightclub. He smiled when I said eighteen and told me that, when he reached eighteen, he wanted to get dressed up and go dancing with me. I laughed and said that most of the women would be a lot older than him. "That's okay," he replied, his eyes twinkling, "I like older women."

We both laughed, but his comment stayed with me. Even though I saw him as Shane, the little boy, I knew he was a blossoming adolescent. Because of the small age difference between us, I wondered if he was confused about his feelings towards me. I certainly didn't want to contribute to those feelings. Perhaps I was relating to him too much as a peer and needed to behave more like an adult and a parent. I thought about this often and decided that continuing to set limits and boundaries was the most appropriate solution.

Shane began to write poetry on the computer, and I encouraged him. He loved to play on my computer, and spent hours writing poetry and letters to his friends. At least he was expressing himself somewhere. He certainly wasn't sharing his feelings with Krissy or me. In fact, he refused to talk about anything remotely connected with emotions unless he initiated the conversation. One of the rare times he talked about his childhood was at the end of a particularly challenging day for both of us.

I belonged to a health club and took Shane in as my guest. We walked up to the desk to check in, and I explained to the receptionist that my son was to be my guest for the evening. She stared at Shane, then stared at me, and stated loudly, "No, he's not."

"What?" I replied.

"He isn't your son," she repeated.

I stared at her and insisted, "Yes, he is my son, and I want a guest pass for him."

She stuttered, "He . . . he can't be your son. You umm . . . don't look like alike, you know."

Then I realized what was going on. I glanced over at Shane, who was carefully studying his Reeboks. I explained that he was my foster son; I was a member in good standing; and he was my guest. Again I demanded a pass. She relented, apologized, and let Shane into the club. I felt so angry. If Shane had been white, she wouldn't have even thought of questioning me. Because he was the first obvious Native American ever to enter this yuppie establishment, she had wanted to filter him out as riffraff.

As we walked towards the locker rooms, I exclaimed angrily to Shane, "Wow, can you believe her?"

Shane shook his head slowly and walked silently into the men's locker room. I sat in the women's locker room for a few minutes, feeling a mixture of anger and sadness for Shane. People were so afraid of the unfamiliar.

While we were at the club, Shane ran into Natalie and her kids. I arranged to have dinner together after our workout. She was a single parent of two children, ages six and eleven. Hoping for a relaxing, family meal, we decided on an Italian restaurant. Shane was quieter than usual, but he began to open up and play with the kids until, suddenly, Natalie blew a fuse and abruptly slapped the youngest child across the face because he accidentally spilled his water. I had never before seen Shane's face register such strong displeasure. His mouth dropped open and he stared defiantly at Natalie, who then looked at me as if to say, 'Don't you dare intervene.' Shane and I quickly finished our meal in silence. As soon as Shane had swallowed his last bite, he asked if we could leave.

Once inside the car, Shane asked me, "Do you like the way she treats her kids?"

"To be honest, I hate it", I replied.

"Natalie is just like my mother," said Shane, "yelling at her kids for no reason. Do we have to go out with them again?"

I hugged him and admitted that it made me really uncomfortable watching Natalie with her children, and we didn't need to be around that. Shane smiled and relaxed, and I dropped the subject. I was glad that he had told me how he felt because I was beginning to worry that he was emotionally shutting down.

As the holidays approached, Shane began disappearing for a few hours after school each day. Krissy punished him by grounding him for one week, but he continued to disappear. One morning about a month before Christmas, Krissy came home Tuesday, after the night shift at the shelter, looking forward to seeing Shane before he had to leave for school, but Shane was nowhere to be found. She called his friends and talked to the neighbors. No one had seen him leave the house. LeRoy, Shane's cousin, had been released from the Juvenile Delinquency Facility a few days earlier, and Shane had started hanging around with him. If he had gone off with LeRoy, they could be anywhere within a five-state area.

As a formality we called the police and filed a missing person's report, although I knew from experience that it wasn't effective. Then I spent a long, sleepless night wondering if his mother had found him and beaten him up, or if he was lying dead somewhere in a back alley.

I showed up at work Wednesday, reluctantly, with deep, dark circles under my eyes, unable to focus on anything but Shane and why he had run away. Every few hours Krissy and I phoned each other, hoping for some news. Nothing. I felt helpless, hurt, and angry.

As the long day crept into a long, dismal evening, full of apprehension, I began to prepare myself for the fact that I might never see him again. He could be anywhere—at his mother's, hiding out with friends, kidnapped, on his way to another state . . . It felt horrible to be living in this limbo.

When Shane finally called Krissy the following afternoon, he acted nonchalantly, like it was no big deal. I was so relieved when I found out he was safe, but was very angry at his indifference to our worry and concern. This was a typical reaction from Shane, minimizing his feelings and any emotions around him; and I found it very irritating and hurtful. Shane called from City Center Mall, where the teens hung out. Krissy rushed over to pick him up and immediately demanded an explanation. The story was that he went to a friend's house and hung out with some kids who passed around booze and little black pills. He didn't know what the pills were and didn't want to take them, but his friends talked him into it by saying they were great. So, he took the pills, blacked out, and woke up in a strange house in northeast Minneapolis. Then he wandered around all day and all night, trying to find his way back home. After hitchhiking downtown, he borrowed a quarter from a wino and called Krissy.

As Krissy drove, Shane dozed off, looking as though he had been dragged through the gutter. He didn't seem to be suffering any major aftereffects, so Krissy took him home, and he slept until Friday evening. When he finally woke up, he wandered around the house with a bad hangover.

Neither of us believed his story; he knew how to call us without using a quarter and had done it before. It was more likely that he got drunk and stoned, then partied till he passed out. He had been raised with such minimal supervision that we assumed he just couldn't handle being responsible for his actions.

Saturday we held a family meeting. The three of us sat down to negotiate his punishment. We wanted his participation so that he would accept some responsibility for fulfilling the terms of the punishment. Three weeks of being grounded with no television was the final decision. He felt it was fair and wasn't upset in the least; it was as if he wanted us to punish him.

The next week's family meeting didn't go as smoothly. By this time Shane was restless and wanted to get out of the house. When Krissy and I mentioned that we felt he was shutting us out of his life, he pretended not to know what we were talking about. I asked him how he felt about our asking these questions and, glaring at me, he growled, "Don't you try to therapize me. I'm not one of your patients."

Speechless for a moment, I replied, "Shane, I can't read your mind. If you don't want to talk to us, then go to a counselor."

"No counselor!" he screamed at me.

I got up and left the room, feeling overwhelmingly frustrated. That was the first time I thought Shane might be more than I could handle.

When I returned to the room, Krissy was telling Shane that the next time he disappeared, he would go into counseling—no excuses. His running away was too hard on us, she told him, and there was obviously something going on that he was refusing to talk about. Shane continued to stare at the floorboards. After a long silence he muttered, "Can I go now?"

We agreed and reminded him that we both loved him. He nodded and shuffled out of the room.

With the holidays coming, Shane wanted a few extra dollars to spend. I called my dad, who agreed to put Shane to work collating and assembling a mailing he was working on. Shane made the arrangements with my father, insisting that he wanted to start work a day earlier than my father had suggested. But on Friday, when I picked him up at Krissy's, his enthusiasm had waned. Sitting on the couch with his arms folded across his chest, he stared sullenly into space. When I ask him what was wrong, he responded that he had made plans with his friends. Exasperated, I explained to him that my dad was counting on him. Dad had told the other worker that he wouldn't be needed that evening. Shane was adamant, "I don't want to do it!"

I knew that if he didn't show up, I would have to do it because Dad was expecting to find the job completed when he arrived at the shop the following morning. After arguing and pleading with Shane for half an hour, trying to convince him to do this job, I finally laid down the law: either work tonight or stay at home. He looked me in the eye and told me he was going out with his friends. I replied that he was grounded as well as being out of a job.

That night I worked until one a.m. doing Shane's job, after putting in a full day's work at the therapy agency. My father never offered Shane another job.

Shane, on the other hand, slipped out of Krissy's house at two a.m. and came staggering back on Sunday afternoon. He faced two more additional weeks of grounding with no television.

December was a difficult month for both of us. I was fighting with my divorce proceedings and battling over various issues with my husband; and Shane was depressed. One snowy afternoon while we were watching black and white movies on television, he told me about the only Christmas that held good memories for him. He was two, and his mother was married to "kind of a nice guy." On Christmas morning Shane came downstairs and unwrapped his present, one of the few times in his life he had received a Christmas present. "It was a gigantic red fire engine—the kind you could sit on and steer; and it had a big old ladder and shined in the sunlight. You know, I can still smell it. My mom was nice to me, too."

I promised him that this Christmas would be his second best, and he smiled.

Two weeks before Christmas we celebrated my birthday. A few days earlier, he and my dad had gone clothes shopping for Shane, and Shane had come home with a huge grin on his face. When I'd pressed him about why he was so happy, he'd given his usual answer: "Nothing."

Rolling my eyes in mock despair, I walked away, shaking my head. He ignored me and began playing on the computer.

Then on my birthday he proudly presented me with an album by my favorite group. Shyly he explained that he had wrapped it at my dad's house so I wouldn't get suspicious. At that moment, all the testing and struggles I had gone through with that boy seemed unimportant. He was worth every agonizing minute!

The following night I arrived home after midnight, having gone out for a birthday celebration with my friend Angela. Shane was already asleep, which was odd, usually he watched television until four or five in the morning. At about four a.m. I awoke and decided to make myself some tea.

The living room, where Shane slept, was dark, so I got up quietly and crept down the hallway. Then I heard him call my name ever so faintly, in a soft, childlike voice. As I went to kneel beside him, I heard him crying. I asked him what was wrong, and he sobbed even louder. Holding him, I waited until his tears subsided, then asked him to tell me what was the matter. He said he felt sad and began to cry again. Eventually, he blurted out that he missed his sisters and wanted them to live with us. I held him and stroked his hair while he continued to cry, knowing that nothing I could say would take away the loneliness he was feeling.

"Do you want to go back to the reservation?" I asked.

First he said yes, then no. Then I asked if he wanted to visit his sisters and he said no. Living with his sisters would fulfill his dream of having a family, I knew. Being shuffled between two households as he was, with no positive male role model, was not the ideal situation. I told him I wished I could make things easier for him, but I didn't know how. We hugged each other and cried—for his sisters, for his painful childhood, and for my helplessness and heartache. We ended up having some hot chocolate, and I felt glad that he had allowed me to give him some comfort.

Following a family tradition, Shane and I spent Christmas at my aunt's house in Wisconsin. When we arrived, my family welcomed him with open arms. There must have been about twelve kids running around the living room.

Santa Claus arrived, and the little ones had their photos taken sitting on his lap. At first Shane sat back and absorbed everything with an eagle's eye, unsure whether to enjoy himself or pretend he was an adult and merely observe; but the kid in him won out, and he wrestled with the rest of the brood. Although he was the oldest kid, Shane didn't seem to feel out of place as he played games with my cousins and stuffed himself with food.

My dad told his nephew John that Shane was his grandson. Astonished, John looked at me and exclaimed, "When the hell did this happen? I never saw this kid before; where's he been hiding?"

Shane and I giggled and gave each other a hug.

The New Year began with a happy heart and a fresh outlook for Shane. He got up on time for school and came home right after school each day. Krissy and I continued to encourage him to express his feelings, without success. Every time we suggested he get help, he became extremely angry and refused to discuss it. Krissy and I agreed that we would wait him out.

It was one of those infamous Minnesota January days, with a wind-chill factor of seventy degrees below zero and icy winds whipping through the cracks in every home. Shane went to bed early that night, which was very unusual. Bedtime always meant a power struggle between Krissy and him. She went to bed but soon awoke to Shane's blaring alarm clock. Reluctantly, she dragged herself out of her warm bed. It was half past two in the morning. Standing in the doorway, she asked him why he wasn't turning off the alarm. No answer. So she reached over the bed, turned it off and staggered back to her room.

A few hours later, she awoke to a silent house. Realizing that she couldn't hear Shane in the shower, she went in to wake him up. He was facing the wall, with his head covered by blankets. When he didn't move after she told him to get up, she tried to shake him, and the lump in the bed separated and deflated. No Shane.

Krissy called me and explained that he had taken his clothes, music tapes, and his savings, which was about sixty dollars. Then she called the school. The administrator was happy to hear from her: Shane hadn't been to school for three weeks, and a truant officer was scheduled to visit her that same day. Krissy couldn't believe it and asked why someone hadn't contacted her before. The administrator explained that they didn't have enough personnel to contact parents every time a child was absent.

We both felt sure that the inevitable had happened—Shane had gone back to his mother. Krissy called Flora and a representative of the Tribal Court. They had expected this from Shane and weren't surprised at the news.

Why hadn't he told us he wanted to live with his mother? I was so tired of worrying about him and trying to read his mind. Neither of us would have forced him to live with us, but he never revealed his true feelings or told us he wanted to leave. I really didn't need all this hassle in my life. I started feeling sorry for myself. None of my friends were going through these struggles of a teenager. If they did have children, the kids were still young enough to listen to adults. I didn't feel like I wanted to end my relationship with Shane, but was very tired of his games.

I was on an emotional roller coaster. I felt angry with him for putting me through this hell; guilty that somehow I could have done more. Maybe, if he had lived with me full-time, things would have been different. I was frustrated and worried, speculating that he had been killed in a street fight, or feared that his mother had killed him, or that he had died from an overdose. Every time the phone rang I dreaded answering it.

The days and nights turned into weeks as Krissy and I blamed ourselves and talked endlessly about what we could have done differently. We reviewed all our conversations with Shane, looking for hidden messages. We called his friends, went through his notebooks, and scanned his computer files. We found nothing. In the end, we conceded that we were punishing ourselves for something we had no control over.

I cycled through the grieving process many times; denial, anger, bargaining, sadness. I blamed Krissy, I blamed myself, and I became bitter. I started to question whether Shane had just been using me, biding his time, until he found his mother.

He seemed to have disappeared off the face of the earth. One night, desperate for a lead, we brain stormed a list of all the friends he had ever mentioned and narrowed it down to Marcie, a girlfriend whom Shane had avoided discussing with either of us. Piecemealing the evidence, we deduced that he had run away with her, and decided to find Marcie.

Driving around the neighborhood, Krissy tried to remember which house she had dropped Shane off at a few weeks earlier. After we had driven up and down several streets and knocked on a few strangers' doors, I began to wonder if Krissy really remembered the house. She described it as a typical middle-class, yellow bungalow with toys in the yard.

Suddenly she stopped the car, jumped out, and ran up the porch steps of a yellow house. A Native American woman in her forties answered the door. Confirming with her that it was Marcie's home, Krissy explained our predicament, and the woman, who introduced herself as Beth, let us in.

Shane visited their home often, Beth commented, listening to music and playing with Marcie's younger brothers and sisters. She thought he was a really nice boy. When I asked if her daughter had run away, Beth responded that her daughter was out partying and hadn't come home for a couple of nights, but that was typical for Marcie. Her mother expressed her concern that she hung out with a bunch of hoodlums. Beth hadn't seen Shane in two weeks, which was near the time he had disappeared, but she did have an idea where he and Marcie might be.

We hopped into Beth's car, which she drove like a maniac, chain-smoking the whole way. Unsure where she was taking us, I was just about to ask her when she squealed up a side street and slammed on the brakes. We piled out of the car and walked up to a dark, ominous-looking house. We had to wait a few minutes before the door was opened by an obese man who stared at us coldly, holding a can of beer. Beth spoke quickly, telling the man about Shane's disappearance. He told her he hadn't seen the kids, then slammed the door in our faces. Although Beth mumbled that the man was probably hiding the kids, I didn't think Shane was staying there.

Silently we rode back to Beth's house, where we climbed out of her car and thanked her for trying to help us. We also apologized for barging in on her, and left quickly. I felt ashamed of myself for involving Beth and making her worry; my obsession with finding Shane was making me irrational. There were other things in my life that demanded my attention, such as my job and term papers due in two weeks.

Although I'd be lying if I said I didn't still think of Shane constantly, I did began to concentrate more on my own life. There was a power greater than all of us, I believed, with a divine plan, and I had to trust that Shane would be safe. Cramming term papers and focusing on my new relationship with James filled my days. James understood and sympathized with me but, like my other friends, felt helpless. Krissy called me occasionally, letting me know that Marlina had been at the shelter looking for me. Shane wasn't with her. Otherwise she wouldn't be after me again. Searching for information at the shelter proved that Marlina was getting desperate to find Shane. She was still banned from the shelter but that didn't prevent her from badgering the staff. Her shelter visits became more frequent, averaging one a day.

I wasn't surprised when Shane called me, based on his modus operandi; when the pressure from his mother was too much for him to handle, he ran from her.

It had been a month since he had run away. He was staying with his cousin LeRoy and was okay; but he had contacted the interim home, spoken with Bryce, and was to return to the reservation that night on the eleven o'clock train. I didn't know what to say. I knew I wanted to see him, so I asked if we could meet for dinner. He agreed and told me to pick him up at Burger King on Lake Street. I asked him several times if he would be there because I didn't want to drive twenty miles if he was going to chicken out. He assured me he'd show up, so I sped over to Minneapolis with a million questions running through my mind, the biggest of all being, 'Why?'

Ironically, as I got closer to the restaurant, I realized I already knew the answers. It's was so apparent to me that I'm humiliated to admit I truly hadn't known. Shane was a highly dysfunctional, abused, chemically exposed child from a family that used him with the utmost disregard; and a culture that really didn't want to take responsibility for him. Were my expectations overly optimistic? Did I cross the line, ignoring professional boundaries? Absolutely! Would I do it again? Okay, I admit I hesitated on that one, but if I thought about my life without Shane in it, it looked like a black void. Yes, I would do it again.

Determined to enjoy the last minutes we had together, I gave him a big hug and sat down facing him. He looked tired, but clean. He told me he had dropped his bag and lost all his clothes when he and LeRoy had run away from a police car that was shining a spotlight on them. When they went back early the next morning, the clothes had disappeared.

He and his friends had been partying, he said, and that was where he ran into his mother. He had moved in with her, but they soon got on each other's nerves, with her drinking and getting crazy. One day she had started hitting him, and Shane, deciding he wasn't going to take it any more, had hit her back. Marlina had told him that if he wanted to fight, she would fight him till he couldn't walk. Shane ran off. Marlina followed him, but he outran her, and he'd been hiding ever since.

Having decided on a restaurant for dinner, Shane told me he'd left his Reeboks in an apartment and asked if we could stop on the way to pick them up. Surprised that he hadn't lost them, I smiled when he teasingly told me he would never lose them because he knew I'd kill him if he did.

Following Shane's directions, I pulled up in front of a rundown apartment building in a neighborhood known for drug dealing and prostitution—very close to where the bullet had gone through my car window. Shane warned me that his mother was staying there, but said she wouldn't be at home this early. He ran up the steps and disappeared into the building. I was fiddling with the radio when I suddenly felt as if I was being watched. Glancing up at the first floor apartments, I saw a hand moving the curtains to one side. As I shifted positions, trying to get a better look, Shane darted out of the building and jumped into the car, screaming, "Move! Move! She's after you!"

Burning rubber, I squealed out into the busy street, while Shane rattled on about his mother wanting to come after me and kill me. In a shaky voice, I asked him if she knew where I lived. Shane had told her I lived in Minneapolis, when actually I lived in St. Paul, but he advised me not to show my face in this neighborhood again or drive my car around here.

"She hates you," he replied, when I reminded him about the time she had been out to get me when he first went to the reservation. I couldn't worry about that now. Shane was leaving, and I wanted us to part on good terms.

We went to my place and gathered up his remaining belongings, then went to his favorite restaurant. None of us were hungry, but we had a couple of hours to kill before Shane's train left. At my invitation, James came with us. I needed a shoulder to lean on, and James helped make the conversation flow. Shane was very quiet and withdrawn. Reality was finally hitting me, and I had trouble talking to Shane without my eyes filling with tears. I was afraid that once I started crying, I wouldn't be able to stop, so I kept the conversation very superficial.

We drove to the train station in silence, each of us in our own world. Luckily, James timed the departure perfectly; we had no agonizing minutes in the depot to say long goodbyes. I promised I would visit him after he was settled. Shane just stared at his feet. The train whistle blew and, for a few awkward seconds, we stood gazing at each other. Shane started to say something, then stopped. He turned to James and hugged him, then began to walk away. I grabbed him, spun him around, and gave him a long, loving hug. "Last call for Wanagi Lake, North Dakota," the loudspeaker bellowed. Shane and I released each other with tears in our eyes. I told him I loved him, and, looking into my eyes, he replied, "I love you, too."

*Are **YOU** okay?*

*Are you **OKAY**?*

People always ask me that.

*I don't think they know
what they're getting into,
So I tell them what they want to hear.*

"I'm fine," I lie.

*What if I told the truth?
They'd wish they hadn't asked me!*

*I'd scream, "No, I'm not okay!
I'm anything but okay!"*

but it wouldn't make a difference.

Shane Lone Eagle

8

Distancing

March

MY LIFE FELT EMPTY AFTER SHANE LEFT. FOR A FEW WEEKS I lived like a hermit, taking time to reflect on the recent whirlwind. Eventually I got back into my old routine of studying and visiting friends on the weekends, but, without Shane, life just didn't seem as rich and fulfilling any more. I had started to see a therapist about my divorce, and the sessions inevitably wound up centering around Shane. During one particularly intense session I talked to Shane's spirit, telling him how much I missed him, even though I knew that being on the reservation was the best thing for him. I expressed how important he was to me and how he had helped me put my life into perspective—I now saw where my priorities lay.

Other emotions jostled for my attention, especially anger over his poor decisions. He had thrown it all away, shattering my high hopes for him. His lack of self-control and his seeming lack of respect for me left me feeling disappointed. Why couldn't he have been honest about his desire to be with his mother? I also felt empty, rejected and used, and wasn't at all sure that I wanted to deal with him ever again.

My feelings mellowed into depression, which lingered like a patch of old dirty snow refusing to melt. I knew it would take time to get over his abrupt departure, and I began to consider staying out of his life permanently. Did my interactions with him benefit or confuse him? My love for him hadn't diminished, and I certainly wanted to be a part of his life, but I felt ambivalent. If his life would be better without my interference, then I would let go of him. I decided to distance myself from him—give him and myself some space to see what happened next.

I lasted a month. My heart ached and I longed to hear his voice, but I knew he wouldn't contact me for fear of rejection. It took me half an hour to get up the nerve to call him at the interim home. After I heard the house parent calling him to the phone, telling him who was on the line, I began to have misgivings: what if he hung up on me or got upset. Maybe this wasn't a good idea.

"Hi, Stranger!" I said lightly. Silence.

My heart beating wildly, I waited until he sullenly replied, "Hi." I stuck to casual conversation about my school and his school, then asked how he was doing.

"Fine," he responded.

"Now tell me how you're really doing," I said.

Another long silence, "Okay."

After a few more attempts, I said I would be quiet and let him do the talking. Shane was silent. Unable to stand the strain any longer, I admitted that I still loved him and wanted to be in his life, but only if he wanted it too.

"Yeah, Deb, I do."

I was flooded with relief. It wasn't until then that I realized I'd been holding my breath. Relaxing, I suggested that I come and visit him, if he wanted me to. He said he did, and we ended the conversation.

Even though we had only been on the phone for a few minutes, it was long enough for some real communication and understanding to take place. Happy that we had reestablished contact, I also felt some sadness. Shane hadn't sounded good—in fact he sounded depressed, and I suspected he wasn't doing well at the interim home. But I had to remember that the situation was out of my control—Shane had chosen to be there.

Now that we had broken the ice, I felt comfortable calling him the following week. We talked about a new girl in his life (he went through girls like a kid opening his Christmas presents), laughed about some of our experiences together, and enjoyed a warm familiarity. After a few months of regular phone calls, I found myself planning a trip to see Shane and his sisters.

James accompanied me, partly to enjoy and explore the area, and partly to help diffuse the energy between Shane and me. Aware that my visit might churn up his emotions and leave him unsettled, I experienced some doubts about going; but I sensed that he was already rebelling and feeling somewhat abandoned by Krissy and me.

As we neared the reservation, my hands started to get clammy and I flashed back to the scene where Shane had warned me not to be his therapist. I hoped that I wasn't walking into one of his mind games and being taken for a fool. I had reached out to him from my heart and traveled too far to deserve that kind of treatment.

The day was sunny and beautiful as we drove through the heart of the reservation and took the road to the interim home. Pulling into the driveway, I glanced toward the house and saw Shane leaning against the door frame. As James wandered around the grounds, I walked up the driveway to meet Shane. Instead of waiting for me, he turned away and walked into the kitchen, where he sat at the table and stared at the tile floor.

We followed him in, and James tried to make small talk. Shane answered in monosyllables and continued to stare at the floor. As James ran out of things to say, I asked Shane what was wrong. He was on restriction, he replied, and couldn't leave the building; actually he wasn't even supposed to leave his room. With that he gave a deep long sigh and went back to staring at the tiles.

When I asked him why he was on restriction he commented that he had run away. Then he admitted that he was thinking about running away again so that he could meet us somewhere and be free to do whatever he wanted. Ignoring his ridiculous idea, I asked him who we needed to talk to get the restriction lifted.

"There isn't anything anyone can do," he muttered, shaking his

88 *Distancing*

head. I insisted that he lead me to the person in charge.

"Minus four hundred," Bryce, the counselor, announced when Shane asked him to count up his points. The interim home used a behavior modification system that awarded points for good behavior and deducted points for bad behavior.

"Is that bad news?" I asked Shane, who had looked away and was shaking his head.

"Hopeless," he replied.

"What would Shane have to do to get permission to leave the building?" I asked Bryce.

After careful consideration, Bryce said that Shane would have to rake the entire front yard, bag the leaves, and sweep the sidewalk.

I looked questioningly at Shane, who stared at me as if I was crazy and whined, "No way! Do you know how long that would take?"

Taking Shane's arm, I dragged him out of the office, telling him it wouldn't take that long with the three of us, and we could make it fun. He shrugged his shoulders, keeping his head down. James asked him where the gardening supplies were kept. Shane gestured with his foot, and we went off to find them. Spending our time trapped in that interim home with a sullen teenager wasn't our idea of a vacation, so James and I grabbed the rakes and trash bags and went outside, leaving Shane behind. Determined not to let Shane's hopelessness affect me, I ignored him.

We had raked a quarter of the yard, making a game out of it, when Shane moved from the doorway and picked up the rake leaning against a tree. Still shaking his head, but letting a smile creep onto his face, he began to rake. James and I threw handfuls of leaves at each other, laughing and being silly, but Shane kept his distance. About an hour later we finished the raking and started to bag the leaves, playfully tossing leaves at each other. A couple of times Shane had begun to join in the leaf throwing and have fun, but he'd remember that he was still in a bad mood and stop himself.

Putting the bags in the dumpster, we asked Shane where he wanted to go. Unable to believe that he was free, he mumbled that they wouldn't let him go. Pushing Shane in front of us, we strolled into the office. To my surprise, Shane's attitude had changed—his spirits had lifted—

and he asked Bryce how many points he had gained.

"Well . . . ," Bryce announced slowly, "you're free to go."

Shane raced to his room, changed his clothes, and grabbed his jacket. Sprinting past us, he told us to jump in the car yelling that he wanted to pick up his sisters at their foster home and take them to the pizza place with us.

On the way to his sisters' foster home, Shane told me that Allana had tried to commit suicide a few months earlier, but was okay now. To me, Allana had always appeared to be the most strong willed of the three, having taken the biggest risk, so I was surprised and upset to hear that she was still struggling with suicide. I hoped there would be an opportunity to talk to her privately, although I doubted it. Shane demanded all my attention.

We drove to Wanagi Lake and the kids chattered and teased each other all the way there. Missy, eleven years old now, was at the stage where she wanted to wrestle with anyone who was willing. More reserved at age twelve, Allana was practicing being a young woman. Shane was like a puppy, leaping on anyone who wanted to play. So, the back seat was jumping during the drive.

At the kids' request we went to a teenage pizza place which specialized in cheeseburger pizza. The kids ordered this disgusting pizza while James and I ordered a basic pepperoni. About twenty kids filled the place, climbing on chairs, yelling, screaming, and behaving like wild monkeys. The noise was unbelievable. James and I had to shout at each other just to be heard.

Shane and his sisters were just as wild as the rest of the kids and couldn't sit still for more than a few seconds. Playing video games, going to the bathroom, kicking each other under the table, and wrestling with each other, they drove us nuts. Under different circumstances, we might have enjoyed it, but having driven for ten hours non-stop, we just wanted to lie down and sleep. Convincing the kids that watching television in our motel room while we caught a quick nap would be fun, we drove the block to the motel and tried to get them interested in cartoons.

But they wouldn't have it. All they wanted to do was wrestle and tickle each other. James lay on the bed staring at the ceiling while the kids screamed and giggled. Thinking they would wind down after a few minutes, I left them alone. Half an hour later, as they got louder by the minute, James and I realized that there was no way we were going to get any rest. As the kids began singing songs as loud as they could, and off-key, James and I splashed cold water on our faces and asked them where they wanted to go.

"Bowling," they cried in unison.

The bowling alley was just across the street, so we walked. Even though James and I were exhausted, we soon felt better and enjoyed being with the kids. They played around with the balls, tripped each other up, and generally tormented each other, as siblings do. It had been a long time since they had been together as a family in a carefree situation. Leaning over to James, I whispered that my dream would be to live with these kids in a farmhouse in the country and have a family life. He nodded, knowing how much I cared about them, and squeezed my hand.

The next day James and I drove to the interim home to find Shane doing his chores. He told us quite cheerfully that he had to clean the living room before he could go anywhere. What a change from yesterday! As soon as he was ready, we went to pick up his sisters, having planned a trip to Wanagi's Heart.

Wanagi's Heart is a large butte overlooking the reservation, which can only be reached by four-wheel drive. According to Shane's version of the legend, a man possessed by evil spirits went to the top of the butte, cut his heart out, and offered it to the spirits. Fearing that this man's spirit will posses them, the Indians don't go up there after dark.

As we started up the rough dirt road, the kids got excited and dared James to drive all the way to the top. Charging through mud holes and melting snow, James reached the base of the butte, where he stopped the truck and asked the kids if they were absolutely sure they wanted to go all the way up.

"Yes, go!" they yelled, and we barreled up the steep grade. Allana started screaming that we weren't going to make it, while Shane laughed and yelled.

Once we reached the top, the girls leaped out, giggling at how scared they were. Shane and I had brought a kite with us and tried to involve the girls in flying it, but they were more interested in going back to the truck and listening to the stereo.

Running to get the kite off the ground, we came upon some sticks wrapped in cloth that had been planted in the earth. Shane explained that they were prayer sticks. While praying, people wrapped tobacco in cloth, tied it to a stick, and dug the stick into the ground. This allowed the prayers, which were now contained in the tobacco package, to reach the Great Spirit and be answered. About a dozen of the prayer sticks dotted the area, and Shane warned me not to touch any of them and to avoid walking close to them.

Still trying to get the kite airborne, Shane and I ran around the top of the butte, but we had no luck. With a determined air, Shane ran down the steep embankment pulling the string behind him, but the wind wouldn't cooperate. He zoomed up and down that butte ten times, laughing and gasping for breath, trying to get that kite to fly, while I sat on the ground watching him play.

Suddenly he stopped and stared into a wooded patch about forty yards away. Moments later, running over to me, he excitedly described the white wolf that had stood silently in the woods watching him. By the time I stood up to look, the wolf had disappeared. I speculated if this was Shane's power animal, who guided him in the spirit world.

Picking up the kite string again, Shane ran and managed to get the kite in the air for a short time, but not long enough to justify all his efforts. James and I watched him running wild and free, without a care in the world. If only Shane's life could be like this all the time, I mused, instead of for a few sporadic moments. This sweet, innocent boy deserved to be happy. As I gazed up into the deep blue sky, thinking about his life, Shane sneaked up, jumped on me, and started tickling my sides. Soon his sisters got in on the act, and I was attacked from all sides. We laughed and wrestled together, having a great time. Life couldn't have been simpler—or sweeter—at that moment.

The next day—our last—we picked up all the kids and Missy insisted we go to her favorite playground in a town near Wanagi Lake. She didn't know exactly where it was, only that it was by a lake, so we drove around the countryside while she gave us directions like, "Oops, turn here," "This looks familiar," and "Back up, I see something."

We did find a playground, but it wasn't her favorite one. In fact, we soon became aware that it was in an all-white community as people started coming out of their houses to stare at us. Not wanting the situation to turn ugly, I suggested we go somewhere else, saying that the town didn't look friendly.

"But I wanted to swing." Missy whined, as we got back into the truck. Shane consoled her—he knew why we wanted to leave—and led us to a playground in Wanagi Lake.

It was a gigantic playground, which we had all to ourselves, with a field to fly the kite and lots of rides. Missy loved it as we pushed each other on the swings and the merry-go-round, while Shane wandered around looking bored. After pushing her on the swings, James followed her to the merry-go-round and spun her around, while she screamed, "Faster, faster."

Spinning at high speed, she reached out for James, lost her balance, and flew off the platform, landing on her tailbone. Before either of us could react, Shane had run over to her and put his arms around her. The wind had been knocked out of her and her elbow was skinned. Holding her bleeding elbow, Shane led her to the water fountain and gently washed off the blood. Soothing and comforting her, he calmed her down. Although he had obviously taken care of his sisters many times before, this was the first time I had witnessed it. Missy responded to his concern immediately and stopped crying.

Every second of the trip was spent entertaining the children and, unfortunately, I didn't have any time to talk to Allana alone. I tried to ease my mind by telling myself that she had a wonderful, nurturing foster mother who influenced her behavior much more than I could, being hundreds of miles from the reservation.

During the brief time Shane and I spent alone, we talked about his life at the interim home. He told me he hated it there. The other kids were too square for him; he was bored; and there wasn't anything to do except get into trouble. His whole attitude changed as he spoke: he clouded with sullenness and depression. I knew that I had to talk to his counselor before I left.

Without being too obvious, I sought out Bryce while James and Shane were playing pool. He told me that Shane wasn't trying to fit in at the interim home. It was as if he had given up hope and was refusing to try any more, he said. City life had changed Shane and he was drinking, using drugs, and dealing drugs at school. I reminded Bryce that Shane had been living with his mother again before coming back to the reservation, and it had probably affected him deeply. Admitting that this might have contributed to his unruliness, Bryce still felt that Shane should have adjusted by now. Rather than argue with him, I thanked him and went back to the pool table, feeling troubled that Shane wasn't doing well.

Dust thrown up by a fierce windstorm blotted out the sun the next morning. Billboards lost their posters and cars had difficulty staying on the road. This would have been a good excuse to stay another day, but James and I had to return to work, so we went to say goodbye to the girls, then drove to the interim home.

Shane was very depressed and his air of hopelessness had returned. I reminded him of all the fun we had had and told him I'd be back for another visit. He could also come to visit me, I told him, but he shook his head, saying that it would be too hard on him.

We hugged each other and waved goodbye, tears welling up in our eyes. As we drove away, tears streaming down my face, I was flooded with all the emotions I had repressed during the visit. Leaving him at the reservation, knowing that he hated it, was the hardest thing I had ever done. And there was absolutely nothing I could do to help him.

Taking turns driving through the windstorm, James and I were lost in our own thoughts. A couple of hours went by, and we began to laugh at things the kids had said and done, and grieve over the pain Shane had to endure. Once again I voiced my dream of raising the kids in a healthy environment. Emotionally, I knew I could do it, but, financially, it just wasn't possible. I was the only person who maintained steady contact with Shane; the other foster homes never worked out, and his relatives wouldn't accept responsibility for him or his sisters. It was frustrating to feel so helpless; and even though James sympathized and supported me, he didn't have any solutions.

After this last visit to the reservation I began to understand why Shane found it so difficult to make the transition between the white world and the Native American world. My world was fast paced and full of tension; his world was like a tranquil stream—slow, steady, but always in motion. Certainly, the reservation has major problems—drugs, alcohol, suicide, and a general sense of apathy—and in many ways it is a prison for the Native Americans. And yet some of the old ways hold much appeal: time doesn't rule people's lives; the pace is much slower; and there is a strong sense of community. With my minimal exposure and glimpse into the Indian ways, I could see that balancing the two worlds without destroying oneself was a real challenge.

The following month at the interim home wasn't an easy one for Shane. He began to take his city influence to heart and deal drugs to his peers. He also ran away twice. Since no amount of punishment or restrictions altered his behavior, Bryce, the counselor, decided to send him away to a juvenile delinquency compound, known as JD Camp, in Williston, North Dakota, a couple of hundred miles north of the reservation. At this point, foster homes were completely out of the question. No sane person would take a child who was this destructive.

Shane and I kept in contact, and he expressed his anger about the decision. He felt that the reservation, and his people, didn't want him any more. It seemed to be true. The tribe was tired of dealing with him, and his behavior wasn't helping his cause. It was a vicious circle. Refusing counseling for problems stemming from his childhood, he continued to break the rules and misbehave. This brought more punishment on himself, which he reacted to by further rebellion and disobedience.

When I asked Shane if he was going to say goodbye to his sisters, he told me he couldn't face them. Of course he threatened to run away, and I pointed out that it wouldn't solve anything, and besides, where could he go? He talked about running to the Twin Cities to live with me, but I reminded him that we'd already tried that, and it hadn't worked. I didn't blame him for wanting to run; his options weren't too appealing. I felt frustrated with the tribe; they were dumping him. It was like watching a nightmare that got worse . . . and worse.

Shane packed his bags again and took the train to Williston. The JD Camp was a Christian home for boys aged twelve to eighteen who couldn't be placed in foster homes for various reasons. Some were sent there temporarily by their parents to scare some sense into them, while others had severe behavior problems and this was the last place they could go. Shane belonged in the latter category. He left the reservation without incident. No one said goodbye. He was alone.

9

Nature Connection

April

NOT WANTING TO CONFUSE SHANE OR CAUSE CONFLICT BETWEEN his living with me or at the Camp, I restrained myself from calling him for a couple of weeks. I knew that he needed some time to adjust to the "prison," although I did worry about him.

I had to call the reservation's interim home to get the phone number and full name of the JD Camp. Laura, the director, came to the phone and acted as if she didn't know who I was, which was peculiar considering I had been there a few weeks earlier. After asking questions about my employment and my relationship to Shane, she revealed that she had been screening me to make sure I wasn't Shane's mother. Shane had left strict instructions that he didn't want his mother to know where he was, and they thought it quite likely that she would try to impersonate me to try to reach him.

Once she was confident that I was who I said I was, the director gave me the phone number, adding that Shane was doing as well as expected. Thanking her, I got the feeling he wasn't coping with the change and immediately called the JD Camp.

I was confronted with the same situation when I asked to speak to Shane. They quizzed me about my relationship to him (not exactly easy to explain) and why I wanted to talk to him. Evidently satisfied with my answers, they transferred the call to his cottage where his house parent screened me again. Each cottage has a resident adult called a house parent who is trained in working with volatile teens and maintains cohesiveness in the home. I could hear Shane's name being yelled through the house and was beginning to regret calling. Before I had time to wonder how he would react to me, he came on the line, answering in a low, sullen tone. I was so happy to have reached him that I ignored his attitude, telling him how good it was to hear his voice.

"Deb, is that you?" he shouted, excitement sending his voice an octave higher. After we had chatted for a little while, I zeroed in and asked him if he was lonely. He said he wasn't. There were lots of kids his own age; and he didn't miss the reservation at all. In fact, the reservation sucked.

He was enjoying the horseback riding and the country setting, and insisted he was happy living there. When I asked him if it was like a prison, he responded that it wasn't like that—it was pretty nice, a lot better than the interim home on the reservation. The point system for behavior modification was used, Shane explained, "But it's easier to get privileges and there's more to do here."

When we said goodbye, I told him to call me any time. Of course he'd lost my number, so I gave it to him again.

I felt a rush of sadness and relief, tinged with guilt and hope. Maybe the JD Camp could save him where I had failed. (Yes, I was still blaming myself.) At the age of fifteen, he was only at fifth-grade level, and I hoped this was his opportunity to make progress with his studies. I wanted him to change his behavior and benefit from what seemed like his last chance.

He was placed into an accelerated learning class at the Camp, which would make up for his years of missed schooling and prepare him to return to public school. He seemed to be adjusting well to the environment, his spirits continued to improve, and he actually sounded cheerful. After each weekly phone call, I missed him more.

Although I invited him to visit me, he still felt that he couldn't come back to the Twin Cities without being tempted to return to his old ways. So we decided it would be better if I drove to Williston to visit him. Steve, who was Shane's counselor at the Camp, thought that seeing me would improve Shane's disposition, and he told me he thought it was a good idea.

Since Williston is a twelve-hour drive from the Twin Cities, James and I decided to take four days off and have a mini-vacation. In the meantime, Shane arranged for us to stay on the Camp, which had a house for the residents' visiting family members. It was strange to think of myself as Shane's mother—I saw myself more as his big sister—but I was beginning to get accustomed to that role.

On a sultry July day that the Midwest is notorious for, we headed west to North Dakota before the sun rose to gain a few hours of cool weather.

The car didn't have air conditioning, so I'm not sure whether the absence of the frequent windstorms was our good fortune or not. Enjoying the contemplative state that arises when driving through the flatlands of the Midwest, we were about two hours behind schedule. Stopping at a drugstore, I left a message for Shane that we were running late, but not to worry. I stressed the importance of his receiving the message because he was expecting us, and the receptionist promised to pass it along to him.

The camp was exactly as I had envisioned it—nestled picturesquely between golden buttes, surrounded by a white picket fence, with horses and sheep wandering the plains.

Signs led us to the largest of twenty buildings. The main facility, which contained offices, staff quarters, a cafeteria, recreation room, and gym, was of contemporary design, and excellently maintained. Small duplexes encircled the main complex, and a quaint church stood nearby.

Having no idea how to find Shane, we pulled into the parking lot and I entered the main complex. The receptionist directed me down a long corridor of closed doors to find his counselor.

"Steve is waiting for you! Just go down there, and you can't miss him." Waving a pointed finger in a vague direction, she dismissed me.

Road weary, tired, and frustrated, I briefly entertained thoughts of avoiding this formality and searching the cottages for Shane. After wandering up and down the corridor, I knocked on the only partially open door and asked a blonde man in his late twenties, sitting behind a desk strewn with open files, if he knew where I could find Steve.

"That's me," he responded.

Managing a smile, I said, "Good, I've been searching for you."

"Well, I've been here the whole time, haven't moved," he quipped.

Since he didn't offer me a chair, even though I must have looked exhausted, I simply asked for Shane's room number. Instead of answering, he began to question me about Shane's past. Why didn't he read Shane's case history, I wondered, but then decided to accommodate him, thinking this might be another screening to determine who I was. When Steve quizzed me about my contact with Shane while he was in Minneapolis, I realized that the JD Camp was pretty much in the dark about Shane. I told him a little of our history and gave him my interpretation of Shane's running behavior.

Taking advantage of a pause in his questioning, I asked him how Shane was doing. "Up and down," was all Steve said.

When I requested clarification, Steve commented that Shane wasn't fulfilling his potential (nothing new there), but they weren't going to push him until he became more familiar with the Camp. With that, he concluded the conversation, and I sensed that he was unwilling to share any information with me. Feeling confused, I left his office wondering if this place would be able to meet Shane's therapeutic needs. The "interview" had left a bad taste in my mouth.

As I emerged from the building, I saw Shane running towards the car where James was waiting. I joined them and put my arms around Shane, trying to conceal my tears. We all wrestled and tickled each other, breaking a potentially emotional moment. Shane had grown about five inches in the past three months; he was taller than me now and reminded me of a daddy-long-legs spider. I couldn't help staring at this young man whose breaking voice sounded hoarse and squeaky at the same time. Shane was a man! Unbelievable.

"Didn't think you were coming," he said, bouncing from one foot to the other.

"You didn't get our message that that we were running late?" I asked in surprise.

"Nope, no one gave me any message," he replied. I was shocked. Knowing that Shane would have been counting the minutes until we arrived, he could have been tempted to run away when we didn't show up on time. That was rude and inconsiderate of the receptionist considering Shane's issues of abandonment.

I apologized profusely, and Shane said that he had been planning to give us another half hour, then run away. Curious to hear his explanation, I asked him why he would do such a thing.

"There would be no reason to stay if you hadn't come," he replied nonchalantly.

That was Shane's way of telling me that he was at the JD Camp because I wanted him there, and if I wasn't going to support him, he'd run away and do whatever he wanted. I made light of his remark and asked him to show us where he lived. Skipping, he lead us the two blocks to his cottage, chattering all the way about the kids who lived there—whom he liked and didn't like—and warning me to watch out for the "kinda dirty" boys.

The comfortably furnished cottage contained a large living room, the boys' rooms, and sleeping quarters for the house parent. About twelve boys lived in each cottage. The counselors assigned cottages according to the boys' behavior. Some of the small rooms were shared by three or four boys, others were singles or doubles. Shane shared his room with three other boys about his age. Still chattering, he showed us the white and gold karate belts he'd recently been awarded. One of his roommates, Donald, who later became his best friend, also practiced karate, and Shane had joined forces with him to "defend ourselves against the big guys."

Distracted by the girlie pin-ups taped to his walls, I barely listened to him. I was definitely uncomfortable with his objectifying women; and the realization that Shane was a man threw me off balance and made me feel uneasy. How do I define my relationship with him? I'm not a relative or someone he grew up with, and I certainly don't feel like his foster mother. The feelings I had for him were unique.

Struggling to bring myself back to the here and now, I watched him and James talk about karate'. What would happen to him? Naive and innocent as he was, he had also seen the cruel and evil side of humanity. He needed therapy to help him delve into that dark pool that made him run. Perhaps this would be the place for him to deal with the issues that made Shane want to self-destruct. Again the question formed in my mind—'What kind of adult will he become?'

My thoughts returned to the present as James was asking Shane if he'd eaten dinner. He leaped up and exclaimed, "Hey, we're missing dinner." Following Shane, we jogged over to the main complex and climbed three flights to the cafeteria.

As Shane strode up three steps at a time, I noticed for the first time what he was wearing. "Preppie clothes!" I teased him and, blushing, he tried to explain that all the guys here wore that style.

"Shane is a preppie," I chanted, and, still laughing, we entered the cafeteria.

I quickly noticed that everyone was watching us; I was the only woman among about two hundred teens and staff members. Wanting to show us off, Shane decided to take the table furthest from the door, so we had to cross the entire room to get there. As we passed each table the boys would stop their conversations and stare, making me feel very awkward. Having claimed our table, we walked back to the food line with Shane telling every adult we passed, including the kitchen staff, "These are my foster parents—all the way from Minnesota–St. Paul!"

He was so proud of us, and he wanted them to know that people cared about him. It was a joy to watch him and share his happiness. I was also proud to be with him and felt honored by his enthusiasm.

The horrible dinner of steamed food was standard fare at the Camp, according to Shane. It was cheap though—two dollars a meal. Shane insisted that we go out for our next meal, to which James and I wholeheartedly agreed. After dinner, we hung around the cafeteria talking and filling Shane in on the news from the big city. James tried to take pictures of Shane and me, but we kept annoying him by monkeying around for the camera.

Shane gave us the grand tour: the bee hives (the Camp canned its own honey), horse pastures, barns, industrial arts building, and the visiting family home. It was actually an apartment with two bedrooms (each containing two beds), two bathrooms, spacious closets, kitchen, dining room, and living room. I asked Shane if he wanted to stay with us, but he didn't have enough "points" to receive that privilege. He helped us settle in before returning to his cottage. I collapsed on the bed, dreams filled with hope and promise for Shane.

We spent the next two days exploring Williston, going to a farmer's market, walking in a beautiful park alongside the river, and just playing and having fun. I always enjoyed being with Shane. The time we spent together rekindled the playfulness I had as a child.

While we were at the market we ran into one of his buddies, a boy about two years older than Shane. As we walked towards his friend, I noticed Shane nervously glancing towards me as I walked a few steps behind him. Puffing his chest out, the friend started to run his eyes over my body, obviously considering me to be Shane's date. Shane immediately set him straight, introducing me as his mother and James as his foster father. The boy backed off, "Oh, yeah . . . umm . . . well, I gotta go."

James and I glanced at each other, smiling. Although Shane didn't explain what he was thinking, he strutted beside us, proud to have protected me from being ogled by his macho friend. My feelings were mixed at that moment— proud that Shane had introduced me as his mother, yet also ambivalent about taking on the role of a teenager's mother. And I didn't want him to feel guilty about trying to replace his mother with me.

Sunday, Shane had to go to church. I was surprised that the staff forced every child to go to the service regardless of their religious background. I think Shane was drawn to his own people's spirituality, but didn't have a clue how to go about practicing it. He had never adopted a specific religion. When I asked him how he dealt with going to church, he told me it was easy—he slept through the service.

James and I took a walk while Shane caught up on his sleep in church. I had just finished reading Richard Bach's *Illusions*[1], and remembered the section on vaporizing clouds. Wanting to experiment, I explained the theory to James. Lying on the grass, we stared into a cloud directly above us, focused our attention on it, and watched it slowly dissolve.

James said his eyes were tearing and he wasn't sure if he was actually influencing the cloud. Some people have trouble concentrating so intensely with their eyes open, so I suggested that he try it with his eyes closed. Struggling for a few minutes, with intense concentration, he succeeded in dissolving a tiny cloud. It was ironic that Shane was sleeping through a religious service, not getting anything out of it, while we were gaining spiritual insight lying in a field watching clouds float by.

"Geez, you guys taking a nap already?" Shane exclaimed when he found us. I explained what we were doing and tried to get him to try it, but he looked at me as if I was crazy and declined.

"Just try it, it really works," I said, wanting to share my excitement with him, but he shook his head, mumbling about adults being weird, and walked away.

It wasn't nearly as difficult saying goodbye as it had been the last time on the reservation. The visit had been really enjoyable, and Shane seemed to be his old self (his old lovable self, that is, not his old sullen self). Leaving in good spirits, we promised to call and write, and left him waving goodbye in the parking lot. Reviewing the weekend's events, James and I both noted that the Camp's Native American population consisted of Shane and one other boy, while the staff and the rest of the boys being predominately white. We both felt concerned about Shane's loss of identity; the pull of his land and his people was very strong, even though he didn't often show it.

My life was hectic for the next few months. I was in the middle of my master's program, tired of full time work and school. Questioning what good a stupid piece of paper would do for me anyway, I was often on the verge of giving up. Up all hours of the night typing papers, I couldn't remember what my body felt like without exhaustion. I didn't have any time for a fulfilling relationship with James. But, with his support, I reluctantly stuck with it. If nothing else, I would be able to say I accomplished an amazing feat. Still I kept in touch with Shane regularly by phone.

Shane's life was no longer stable. One Saturday in June he called me, describing how he almost had drowned on a fishing trip when his buddies threw him overboard. Eventually realizing that he couldn't float, his best friend had rescued him.

In midsummer James and I made the long drive to Williston. Not very excited at the prospect, I had urged Shane to visit me, but he refused to return to Minnesota. Although I dropped the subject, I did remind Shane that it was a very long drive. In retrospect, I was glad that I made the trip.

Shane was different. The euphoria he had exhibited last time was absent. Complaining about the counselors and constantly getting into trouble, he said he was bored and seemed generally unhappy. Our activities were limited because Shane was confined to the Camp for fighting, so we spent our time on the grounds. With Shane unwilling to discuss any real issues, our conversation remained superficial. I left feeling disturbed, wondering if he was getting ready to do something foolish. He was a pressure cooker ready to explode.

Our telephone conversations dwindled. He rarely called me any more, and, although I tried to keep up the calls to him, my hectic schedule was pushing him out. Then intuition told me I had to see him and, glancing at my calendar, I noticed that his birthday was around the corner. I called to ask him if he had any plans. He didn't, so I suggested that James and I come and celebrate his birthday with him. Not sounding very enthusiastic, he agreed.

The leaves were turning golden yellows, reds, maroons, and browns on a beautiful fall day. It was unusually warm for the middle of October, so we drove with the windows down. Perhaps we were just getting used to it, but the trip didn't seem to take as long as usual.

Arriving at the Camp, we expected Shane to be waiting for us, but he was nowhere in sight. After wandering around, asking other kids if they knew where he was, I ran into a house parent who told me he'd gone roller skating.

"Didn't Shane know we were coming?" I asked.

He said Shane had expected to be back in time for our arrival. What a change from the other visits.

About twenty minutes later Shane strolled slowly towards us. He'd grown another two inches and was now six feet tall, but still skinny as a rail and lanky. Awkwardly we stood and made small talk. Why did we all feel so uncomfortable? Perhaps his maturity had changed the dynamics between us. I knew how to relate to children, but he was a young man now.

A few weeks earlier I had gone for a past-life reading on my unusual bond with Shane. The psychic referred to a time in the 1800's when I, as a Caucasian female, was steering a covered wagon alone through a mountain range in the Southwest. A group of young Sioux men surrounded me, took control of the wagon, and captured me. Unintimidated by their antics, I remained calm, maintaining my pride and dignity. The men were surprised by my composure and lack of fear, which was so unlike the reactions of other women they had captured.

A young brave—Shane—rode very close to the wagon to look at me. As our eyes met, we became physically and spiritually drawn to each other. The brave immediately took me as his "prize," although my strength and determination confused him. Holding my head up high, I maintained eye contact with him, which made him curious. He wasn't accustomed to such behavior; women bowed their heads and were never so bold.

Approaching the tribal elders, Shane asked that he and I be allowed to become life mates. The request was highly unusual because I was not of their blood. After careful consideration the elders allowed the ceremony to take place. Our life together had been a long and happy one.

That reading gave me another perspective on the strong feelings I had for Shane—not sexual attraction, but a deep spiritual bond. In spite of my ambivalence, it was a parent-child bond that held Shane and me together in this life. Perhaps we had been together in other lives also, in different relationships. That might explain my uncomfortableness when his friend identified me as his date. Whatever it was, and however it had grown, the power of this bond astounded me.

Although Shane was once again on restriction, I persuaded Steve to allow him to leave the grounds as long as we accompanied him. I asked Shane how he always managed to be on restriction when we arrived, and he explained that this time he had been set up by the other kids, who were jealous because he was doing so well. The house parents knew he'd been set up, but punished him anyway. Shane had no choice but to accept it.

While James escaped to take a much-needed nap, Shane showed me his new room. Now he had only one roommate, Donald, which meant that his behavior had improved since our last visit. Calling him nerd a few times, Shane made it clear that he didn't like his roommate much, but he explained that he also felt sorry for the kid.

Shane showed off his new clothes, music cassettes, and the black light that he'd bought with his allowance from the Camp; but I could tell that something was not quite right. Avoiding my inevitable questioning and probing, I put energy into planning his sixteenth birthday instead.

Shane's birthdays had usually been dismal affairs, spent alone among the other lost children in institutions of one sort or another. True, a cake had been made for him, but it was having people around who cared that made a difference between having a great or lousy birthday.

Having finally resolved the argument over whether we were dining in or out, we settled on a dinner in the Visiting Family House of macaroni and cheese, fried chicken, soda, baked potatoes, and chocolate birthday cake with white icing. James and I cooked dinner while Shane watched television. He was unusually moody, but I attributed it to birthday blues (I knew he was wishing his sisters were with us) and it being our last day together.

Slumped in his chair, Shane picked at his dinner. When I asked him if he was hungry, he muttered "Yeah, kind of," and continued to pick at the food. Eventually, he'd eaten most of his food except the baked potato, which he had insisted on us preparing for him. I was losing my patience and told him that he had asked for the potato, I had prepared it, and it was on his plate, so he had to eat it. Then I turned away from him and talked to James.

A few minutes later Shane got up from the table, leaving the potato untouched. I told him he couldn't leave the table until he'd eaten it. Glaring at me, he mumbled under his breath, "You can't tell me what to do."

Willing to compromise, I encouraged him to eat half of it, adding that then we could have the birthday cake. He sat down again, but with his body turned away from the table, and covered his eyes with his hands. I couldn't believe it; we'd never had this kind of power struggle before. I wasn't really surprised, just disappointed, because I had wanted Shane to have a birthday he'd always remember. He'd probably remember this one, but not for the reasons I'd had in mind.

After fifteen minutes of silence, James started laughing at the ridiculousness of the situation. I began laughing too, but Shane couldn't see the humor in it. Throwing the potato in the garbage can, he stormed into the living room and turned the television on full blast. Giving him time to cool down, we cleaned up and washed the dishes.

"It's time to cut the cake, Shane."

Silence.

"Shane, you want a piece of cake?"

Silence. Then slowly he dragged himself over to the table, blew out the candles and cut the cake. We tried to make the best of the situation, but James couldn't take it any more and began teasing Shane: "You look like a mad dog. Are you going to bite me?"

After a few minutes of this, Shane smiled in spite of himself; James began to mimic Shane, who proceeded to mimic James, until they were both laughing. With the ice broken, I grabbed the camera, and they posed for me, making clown faces.

I apologized to Shane for trying to force him to do something against his will, and we spent the remainder of the evening watching television. Shane was quiet, though, only answering if spoken to.

I walked him to his cottage and explained that I felt bad about the evening ending the way it had. He stared at the ground, not saying anything. I kept talking, hoping to reach him somehow. "Birthdays can be hard, especially when you want to be with your family and they're not around."

He remained silent, so I carried on, asking him if he wanted to leave the Camp. "Yeah, this place sucks," he proclaimed.

"You could always come back to live with me" I told him, "Maybe things would be different now."

Shaking his head, he said, "How do you know what I'm feeling when I can't even figure it out?" I laughed and reminded him that I had been a teenager myself not so long ago.

I reached out to him and we hugged, both starting to cry. He ran into the cottage, and I walked back to our apartment, letting the tears flow. When he needed help, I felt so helpless. He, too, learned the intimacy dance; wanting to be close, yet backing away from it when love came within reach.

As crazy as it sounds, I was actually reevaluating my life and considering asking Shane to live with me again. Deep down I knew that, unless he worked through his issues with his mother and father, he'd sabotage anything that represented family life to him. Remembering how difficult it had been when he lived with me before, I asked myself, 'How could I go through that again? Did I want to go through it again? Did I really have a choice?'

A few weeks later Shane called me sounding very excited. The Camp was arranging a potential foster home; there were children his age, and it was on his reservation. Having pondered Shane's living situation daily since I got home, I was still very doubtful about having him live with me. Now the problem was resolved, and I was very relieved. He had visited the foster family a few times on the weekends and he really liked them. I told him I was happy and hoped it worked out.

Unintentionally I made Shane choose between spending Christmas with me or his new family. Over Thanksgiving I came up with the idea of Shane coming to visit me for Christmas. He thought it was a great idea; he had enough points, was behaving well, and didn't seem concerned about returning to the Twin Cities. When I asked him how he'd feel if he ran into his mother, he was pretty sure he'd be able to handle it. Hanging up the phone, he promised to call me as soon as had talked to his counselor, Steve, about the visit.

After a few days I began to wonder what had happened; usually he'd call me the next day if he had good news. Assuming something was wrong, I was nervous about calling him, but I had to know what was going on. Apparently Steve felt that Shane should spend his vacation with his foster family because they were setting up the placement, and there was really no reason for him to come to Minnesota.

Shane was upset. He didn't like people controlling his movements. Although I was disappointed, I understood Steve's reasoning and explained it to Shane, encouraging him to enjoy Christmas. Promising to call me on Christmas Day, he hung up, leaving me feeling sad and selfish. I really wanted him around for Christmas. Holidays were always stressful for me and he provided a buffer. I could busy myself with Shane and not worry about the other issues in my life, such as my career, my recently finalized divorce, and my future with James.

A week before Shane's vacation, I called him, and he was still upset about not spending the holidays with me. Reminding him to call me on Christmas Day, I urged him to make the best of it and enjoy his holiday.

On Christmas Day I surprised myself by actually anticipating his call. It was a quiet Christmas for me. I chose to spend the day alone, with James coming over in the evening. Shane never called. I was angry and very disappointed, still struggling with the fact that ours was not a reciprocal relationship. I had never experienced an individual who took the compassion and caring offered from me, but didn't give it in return. This is why I didn't have any children, I wasn't ready to offer complete unconditional love. I still expected something from Shane. I repeatedly had to relearn the lesson that Shane didn't have the same values or expectations as I had. This was very frustrating for me.

Shane spent the spring preparing for his foster care placement, and I spent it studying and working on my thesis. Actually the timing of the placement couldn't have been better. I was already under a lot of stress, and there was no way I could have handled his living with me at that point. We talked on the phone periodically, and he continued to be optimistic about the placement. Perhaps it was taking such a long time to be finalized, I thought, because of his past behavior—the foster family wanted to be sure they could handle him.

Late one evening Shane called in a very peculiar mood. Something was on his mind, but he couldn't bring the problem up. Eventually he told me that his foster parents were being weird. They wanted him to marry a girl he was dating. My first thought was that she was pregnant, but Shane denied it. According to the parents, he spent so much time with her that he should marry her. Again I asked him if she was pregnant, and he responded with an emphatic "No," then added, "The foster parents are Catholic."

What that had to do with anything, I didn't know. I told him it didn't make sense to me. He admitted he was having sex with her, but I knew that, at sixteen years old, he needed marriage like a hole in the head.

Phrasing my questions carefully, not wanting to alienate myself or the foster parents, I asked him if he wanted to marry her.

"No way, I'm too young," he replied. I agreed and told him the whole thing sounded bizarre to me.

"What happens now?" I asked.

Shane quietly responded, "Well, if I don't marry her, they won't accept the foster care placement."

Thinking I must have misunderstood, I asked him to repeat what he had said.

"If I don't marry her, they won't accept me or want me any more."

I asked him how he felt about this, and he replied, "It sucks."

"Was there anything else?" I asked.

"No. That's it."

I tried to support him without tearing down the foster parents, which was difficult. They had already given him his own room in their home; they had purchased clothes for him; and he had made friends in the neighborhood. Something else had to be going on, I thought. I'm not saying that Shane was lying—perhaps he wasn't telling me the whole story. He asked if he could visit me, and I told him I was leaving with James for the Rockies and Glacier Park. I promised he could visit after we got back. He sounded somewhat happier after that.

Our trip gave me time to reflect on Shane's roller-coaster life. Why do some people have drama and trauma every day of their lives? He was certainly one of those souls, and I seemed to be the balancing rod for him. Obviously something had happened between Shane and his foster parents. Either Shane wasn't willing to look at his actions, or truly didn't know what he had done wrong.

Traveling through the mountain ranges, I thought about Shane a lot and hoped he would be able to see the mountains some day. The power and strength they embodied might help him to envision the overall mission of his life rather than the day-to-day struggles.

It was during this trip that I realized I wanted to know more about Native American spirituality. I made a commitment to myself to locate a teacher who would be willing to help me experience a sweat lodge and undertake a vision quest. I had been interested in this subject for a while, but now the pull felt stronger.

My experience in the mountains was so wonderful that I called Shane as soon as I got back. I described the majestic scenery and explained my idea about the power of the mountains being able to somehow calm his senses. The Great Spirit must have heard my plea, because within three weeks Shane told me he and four other boys from the Camp had been chosen to go on a trip to the Tetons and Glacier Park. They were leaving the following morning.

He called me at various times during the trip. One day he stumbled off a mountain cliff and skinned his knee. But most of his calls were about the incredible beauty of the mountains. He watched the animals and described how exciting it was to watch them free and in the wild, and how vast the earth looked from high in the mountains. He was like a little boy. It was a fantastic trip for him, full of beauty and wonder. This was the beginning of good things coming his way.

10

The Pipe

May, the following year

WHY IS IT THE LATE-NIGHT PHONE CALLS ARE WHAT WE remember most? Is it because suddenly leaving the dream realms and reentering the "real" world leaves us vulnerable? When Shane called me at about midnight, I was shocked to hear his voice. Awakened from a deep sleep, I didn't know if it was day or night. I immediately asked him what was wrong because his voice sounded hoarse, as if he'd been screaming. He quietly explained that he'd tried to hang himself—in fact, he had tried four or five times, but hadn't been able to jump clear enough of the chair for the impact to be successful. His throat hurt and his neck was sore.

How could I respond? What should I say to him? If I said the wrong thing he could hang up on me at any moment. His voice was too calm, too detached. I was afraid I wouldn't be able to reach him, to stop the craziness that had possessed him.

After finding out that no one in his cottage was aware of his suicide attempt, I knew I had to convince him to wake up his house parent and tell him about it. He refused, claiming they would put him away, as they had with his friend who had attempted suicide a few weeks earlier.

Thinking that he may have injured his throat, I used that as a reason for his telling someone, and I begged and pleaded with him to confide in them. It took over an hour to convince him that he wouldn't be locked up, considered crazy or a failure, and that he had to tell an adult. I bargained with him, promising he could live with me. I reminded him of how awful it would be for his mother and his sisters if he killed himself.

My professional experience dealing with suicide calls helped me to remain detached. If the reality had set in that this was Shane I was talking to, I don't think I could have done such a thorough job. We ended the conversation with him promising to call me back as soon as he'd talked to his house parent. I threatened to call his counselor if he didn't call me back.

He did call me, extremely upset because they wanted to take him to the hospital for a check-up. The staff called it standard procedure. Shane threatened to run away as soon as we hung up.

"Running away wasn't the answer", I explained, as I persuaded him to go along with them.

"I'm not crazy," he said repeatedly.

Agreeing with him, I tried to explain that every institution has its rules that must be obeyed.

Promising him that I would be in Williston by the end of the day, I hung up the phone and felt—nothing. I was ice cold and numb. James held me and rocked me as I told him what had happened. It was as if I was falling from the top of a tall building. I had never imagined life without Shane and couldn't do it now. So many of my thoughts and actions revolved around him. All I knew was that I had to be with him, get into his mind, tell him how much I cared, and give him strength and support.

Three hours later, I was packed. I had called my supervisor, Robert, with a vague promise to be back in a week; and made a list of phone numbers for James to contact. The final class of my master's degree program was that evening, but I would just have to miss it. Right before I left, I contacted the hospital to make sure Shane hadn't run away. They wouldn't let me speak to him; they had placed him on suicide watch in a locked ward.

The trip that normally took ten hours, I made in seven, driving non-stop as fast as I dared with the music blasting. It seemed to take forever, and my attention drifted from the road so many times that I worried I'd lose control of the car.

You know how, when you're in a hurry, something always seems to slow you down? Well, in Williston that day, there had been an explosion at one of the industrial plants, and ammonia had leaked into the air, covering the town. Three-quarters of the town had been closed down by the authorities: roads, restaurants, and schools; and all public places had been evacuated. Luckily the hospital was at the furthest edge of town from the plant, and I could reach it by driving along the outer roads.

I finally arrived at the hospital, having spent about an additional hour on my detour. Following the yellow lines to the psychiatric ward, I wandered down long corridors until I came to a dead end. Two steel doors blocked the yellow line and a sign on them read, "Psychiatric Ward. Authorized Personnel Only. Locked Facility."

I pressed a buzzer and the door was soon opened by an orderly, who asked the purpose of my visit, then led me to the nurses' station. Walking past a patients' lounge, I glanced at the people watching television there. Some were pacing the floor, others were mumbling and gesticulating. One man who appeared to be in his fifties was yelling and screaming at an invisible entity to the right of him. God forgive me, what had I gotten Shane into? He didn't belong in here, this scene from *One Flew Over the Cuckoo's Nest*.

Of course I wanted to see Shane immediately, but the head nurse wouldn't allow it. After explaining to her why I was there, she referred me to the staff psychiatrist. He briefly updated me on Shane's condition—which was stable—and told me I could visit Shane for only a short time. Visiting hours, he explained, were twenty minute-sessions, three times a day. Once I had explained that I was the only family member who would be visiting Shane and that I had come from Minnesota to be with him, the psychiatrist extended the visiting period to seventy-five-minute sessions, but still insisted that I leave the premises and return each morning, afternoon, and evening. Disgruntled, I reluctantly agreed, and the nurse led me to Shane's room.

When I asked the nurse why Shane was in an adult ward, she explained that it was the only locked facility in Williston. There were four other adolescents in the ward, but because Shane was on suicide watch, he wasn't allowed to associate with them.

Shane was huddled in a fetal position on his bed. He looked so sad and afraid, his eyes were the sizes of saucers, revealing his fear. Thin, with dark circles under his eyes, he squeaked out a "Hi" and shifted his eyes away from me. For a few seconds I was speechless. This was my first time in a psychiatric ward, and my emotions were finally catching up with me. I began to feel as if I were being sucked into in a dank pool of water . . . Trying to focus on Shane, I snapped out of it. Then I talked fast, knowing he would tune me out after a few minutes. I told him how sorry I was that he felt he wanted to die. Then I told him about the time I had tried to commit suicide.

It had happened when I was an undergraduate in my early twenties. Fed up with roommates who didn't clean up their messes or pay their share of the rent, I was living by myself. My small apartment was on the ground floor of an old mansion. The area was gradually being converted from a drug-infested neighborhood full of alcoholics to a yuppie college neighborhood. During this transition phase, rents were still cheap, but the old undesirable neighbors still hung out in the alleys and on the street corners.

I loved my apartment with its hardwood floors, fireplace in the parlor, and large windows facing the street. Other students filled the remaining apartments in the building.

A month after I had moved in and was feeling fairly safe, someone broke in, in the middle of the night, and raped me. I called the police to report the rape, went to the hospital for an examination, and returned to my apartment, assuming I'd just continue to live my life the way I had before.

One week to the day of the rape, the rapist broke into the side door of my apartment and raped me again. This time I had a butcher's knife next to my bed. I picked up the knife and held it against his back while he was penetrating me. I tried to force myself to stab him, but I couldn't do it. I knew that, if I stabbed him, I would never be the same again.

Something inside me would also be killed, and I would never be able to get it back. What that 'something' was doesn't have a word in the English language. Innocence? The soul's essence? The spirit of life? None of these specifically describe what I would have lost, but I deliberately chose being raped a second time rather than take his life. Quietly placing the knife under the bed, I prayed that I wouldn't be damaged, psychologically or physically.

After he left, I called the police again, underwent another painful physical examination at the hospital, and returned to my apartment to pack. I would never live there again.

While I was packing, I found some speed an old boyfriend had inadvertently left behind. I didn't use drugs—I'd never felt that strong of a need to escape—but as I stared at the tiny white pills, I decided that now was the time to escape, for good. Putting about twelve pills in my mouth, I chased them down with some J & B Scotch on the rocks (my drink back then) and settled down in my favorite chair to die.

Some say I should have died, consuming that much speed and alcohol. All I remember is seeing a tunnel with a faint white light at the end of it. As I felt myself being wrenched closer and closer to the end of the tunnel, and the white light became more brilliant by the millisecond, a voice demanded, "Do you want to leave? Are you finished with your work?"

Hesitating for just a second, I screamed, "No, I'm not ready to leave, but what do I have to live for?"

The voice repeated the question, and I yelled, "No, don't let me leave, I'm not ready." Suddenly I was being drawn backwards through the tunnel, the light was becoming fainter and fainter, and I began to cry.

My body jumped, as if an electric shock had gone through it, and I opened my eyes, squinting at the dimmed light in the living room. I glanced at the clock, an hour or so had gone by. Only I knew what had just taken place—I never told my friends or my family. There was a reason I had been put on Earth, and I made a promise to myself to find out why.

Not wanting to give Shane any new ideas for suicide attempts, I didn't elaborate on the specific details, but I did explain that, at that moment, suicide seemed like the most logical, sane thing to do. There were no thoughts of the people I would leave behind or of whether I would go to heaven or hell. Life had suddenly became so unbearable that death was the only thing that could comfort me, and I didn't want to wait around to die from natural causes.

I struggled for the right words or phrases to prevent Shane from another attempt; and by sharing my suicide attempt with him, I feared that I somehow made it okay for Shane to attempt suicide again.

Studies later proved that teenagers wanted someone to talk to them about why they want to do it, to acknowledge and figure out why the feelings were there. Stephen Levine[1], an author of books on death and dying, encouraged this type of dialogue, stating "You have to come from your own broken heart".

Shane gave an understanding smile, then began to talk about his feelings of loneliness, about wanting his mother, yet knowing how hopeless it was. I told him to listen carefully because I really wanted him to understand what I was about to say.

"Shane, if you decide to die, I can't tell you whether that's the right thing to do, because I really don't know. I can only say that I love you very, very much; and whether you are alive or dead I will love you just the same. Should you choose to leave this world, I can't control you, even if I wanted to. I certainly want you here by me, alive, but I won't be angry with you if you decide you can't go on living."

We hugged each other, and Shane responded, "I know what you're trying to tell me. I love you, Deb."

I heard the sound of a throat being cleared in the hallway. The nurse was waiting to escort me out of the ward, and, promising I'd be back in the afternoon, I reluctantly left him.

Shane and I both became accustomed to the patients on the "mental ward," as he called it. He was put on anti-depressants, which I objected to because of Shane's predilection for drugs. But the psychiatrist completely disregarded my concern, possibly because I wasn't a relative of Shane's, and continued to medicate him.

The combination of Shane's depressions and the medication's effects made Shane indifferent and indecisive. He didn't have any strong feelings or really care about anything. Getting him to decide what he wanted from McDonalds was a major undertaking. He refused to go outside for walks, even though the staff encouraged us to get a break from the ward.

My days consisted of waiting for the seemingly few minutes we would spend together, watching the time fly by, and then waiting again. I was in a limbo of sorts—calling my office for messages, hearing the urgent plea for my return to work, and sitting in restaurants killing time; by now the ammonia scare had dissipated. Shane and I watched television together, ate together, and played all of the many board games in the ward. I tried to put some distance between Shane and his suicide attempt. I was hoping he would come to see that life was worth living. This was a challenge, especially on the psychiatric ward with adults laughing hysterically like hyenas, and violently screaming at their own private demons.

I contemplated Shane's life, which was wrought with torment. Caught between the white world and native world; confusion reigned in his heart. He loved the city life, thriving on the fast talk and flashy dress, and so did I. Yet when he was in the city he became agitated and self destructive. On the reservation he was bored with the slower paced lifestyle. Thinking a family would help him fit into society, perhaps ease his painful memories, he was intrigued with me, but he never truly convinced himself. How does one live in both worlds without sacrificing dignity, responsibility and compassion? Shane kept at it, flipping from each world, but wasn't truly happy in either. Where did he belong?

I observed this happening to many minority cultures. I frequently worked with parents about their confusion with their teenagers and young children. I previously assumed it had to do with assimilation. First generation immigrants desperately wanting to be Americans, throwing their children into a society that devours their children. But, in thinking about Shane's case, his people were not first nor even second generation.

According to the Centers for Disease Control and Prevention[2], from the years 1952 to 1992, the incidence of suicide among adolescents and young adults (less than 25 years old) made suicide the third leading cause of death for that age group. 59 percent of young people, in a 1994 Gallup Poll[3], said they personally knew a teenager who had attempted suicide. Shane was depressed, frustrated, had limited coping skills, but I was permanently in his life. There was a deeper issue that I couldn't address, hopelessness. Shane could not see any solution to his problems. As the executive director of the American Association of Suicidology, Alan Berman, Ph.D., stated[4] "...being depressed itself is not a sufficient cause to lead to or explain suicide, hopelessness is a much more abject way of thinking and feeling."

According to *The Prevention Researcher 1996*,[5] the suicide rate among Native American youth is ten times higher than white youth. The transitions between reservation life, boarding school, and outside the reservation, contribute to the high suicide rate. These environments have incongruous expectations placed upon its population, causing stress and anxiety among the Native Americans. Studies have reported that Shane's ethnic group has the highest rate of suicide in this country, and Shane had less than a 50% chance of reaching his 20th birthday. The Native Americans watched their cousins, nieces, nephews, sons and daughters literally disappear before their eyes. Some say the race is dying out, taking their young first.

Looking at the issue from a psychological standpoint, I would be negligent not to investigate Shane's relationship with the worlds in which he lived in. Charles Eppinger, author of *Restless Mind, Quiet Thoughts: A Personal Journal* [6], addressed this concern with his son's suicide. Just as Shane was struggling with two dissimilar worlds, so was Charles' son, Paul, trying to find a balance between working and maintaining his spirituality.

Five days quickly passed and I had to leave. It was extremely painful for me, and I was terrified for Shane. Saying goodbye to him that time was the most difficult thing I had ever done. I had a sense that this would be the last time I would ever see him, but I could tell that he thought I was overreacting as I walked away from him, sobbing. Still, he was the one on anti-depressants, not me.

We returned to our separate lives. I worked overtime, trying to catch up on all the things that had been put on hold. Shane returned to the Camp and continued taking the anti-depressants, remaining aloof and detached.

Ironically, after enduring such a heart-wrenching experience, my quest for a Native American spiritual teacher was easily accomplished. A small bookstore in Dinkytown (a neighborhood close to the University of Minnesota Twin Cities Campus) offered several classes on Sioux Culture taught by an Oglala Sioux, EagleHeart. He shared his philosophy on spirituality, made comparisons with Christianity, and explained basic ceremonies like the vision quest and the sweat lodge. During one of the sessions a fellow student commented that she already had a sweat lodge constructed on her acreage west of the Twin Cities. We convinced EagleHeart it would be an honor for us to have him conduct the ceremony.

As I drove the forty-five miles from St. Paul to Long Lake, the site of the 'sweat,' a rainbow appeared in the sky, and off to the west a cloud formed into a Buffalo head while another took the shape of an eagle in flight. The sky seemed to be telling me I was where I was supposed to be. I was ready.

Nervously, I walked clockwise around the outside of the sweat lodge and slowly crawled into the representation of Mother Earth's womb. The darkness was absolute as we settled our bodies in the small area, being careful not to get too near the fire pit. The first set of heated stones entered the pit, and pairs of eyes became visible all around me. The eyes glowed and danced to the faint drumming of EagleHeart. Then they slowly faded, and I saw myself dancing with a young brave in a ceremony. I had long, black, braided hair and wore a tan buckskin dress. I immediately recognized this as my past life with Shane. Gazing at his young face, I saw that he was crying. He turned and smiled at me. The vision faded.

The second phase of the sweat lodge, called endurances, was equally powerful. Sparks flew out of the stones like fireworks, making a snapping sound. The sparks danced around our bodies before disappearing towards the top of the Lodge. Lowering my eyes, I saw a white light shaped like a five-pointed star skip over my right knee. It glowed and pulsated as it moved around my body. I looked away from the star and my eyes encountered a white, penetrating light like a laser in the distance. The light focused on my left eye, entered my pupil and pulsed power into my brain. Instantly there was only blackness; then I felt the sensation of a small animal hopping up my left arm. All of a sudden, eagle claws appeared over my head. The eagle took me on its wings and flew me over the hills and valleys. I became the eagle and saw the earth through its eyes.

The third endurance gave me a powerful gift, although I didn't know it at the time. A peace pipe floated in front of me, remained stationary for a couple of seconds before spinning in a clockwise circle. Compared to the previous visions, this one lasted a long time. Although the Lodge was completely black, I saw the pipe clearly. Feathers hung from the long stem, and the bowl was small.

The vision of the pipe affected me deeply, and I left the Lodge in a state of confusion. I was dazed and frightened—of what I didn't know. Something had happened to me and I felt really shaken.

I was embarrassed to ask EagleHeart the significance of the pipe vision in case he thought I was bragging about my big, important vision. Trying to minimize the vision, I told myself he'd probably comment, "Yea, people get those all the time."

Catching him leaning against an oak tree, munching on roast turkey from our potluck, I casually asked him the meaning of seeing a peace pipe in sweat lodge. I fretted he'd either say it was no big deal or tell me I'd be dead in thirty days.

At first, EagleHeart assumed I was referring to the pipe that we had loaded with kinnickinnick (tobacco) before the sweat lodge. When I explained the pipe vision, he stared at me with a strange look on his face. I prepared myself for the worst.

He spoke softly and slowly, "It's an honor to have a peace pipe sent to you from the spirit world. It's a powerful vision. You're a very spiritual person. You must be strong."

I felt faint and tried to gather my thoughts while EagleHeart asked me questions about my job and my home. He then asked if I owned a peace pipe.

"No," I replied. "I've thought about a peace pipe, but haven't wanted to purchase one—I don't want to exchange money for a pipe."

"You must make one then," said EagleHeart, and proceeded to describe the pipestone he had at his house, from which I was welcome to choose a piece the next day. I barely heard him.

The next day while getting dressed for work, I noticed odd markings on my arms—three circular groups of small bruises traveled up my right arm. Remembering the sweat lodge, I tried to scold myself for getting hung up on what may be hocus-pocus, but the markings made me nervous. I wanted a practical person's opinion, so I showed the marks to my friend while we were having dinner.

"Looks as if a bird ran up your arm." she commented.

Eight days after my vision I found myself standing in EagleHeart's garage selecting stone for my pipe. Pipestone, a soft red clay-like material similar to sandstone, is carved into a pipe and becomes a portable altar used in ceremonies and rituals. The stone I selected was small in comparison to others, but I didn't want a gigantic pipe that would be uncomfortable to hold. EagleHeart's twenty-one-year-old son Chris was there that day, and he taught me how to use the tools. Mine was the first pipe he had ever worked on. He was as excited as I.

The saw blade became dull almost immediately, so I rushed to the hardware store to stock up on blades. It wasn't until the clerk asked me what I was working on that I realized my face and shirt were covered with a fine layer of pink pipestone dust.

Feeling unable to tell the truth, I stumbled for an explanation and answered evasively, "I'm working on a project."

He laughed and commented on the dust. I smiled, and quickly left the store. For me this was the first of many experiences of balancing the white American world with the Native American spirit world—something Shane had been struggling with for years.

So far I had a crude image of a pipe. One side of it was thin and unevenly angled. Chris told me I wouldn't be able to sand this side to a smooth finish without damaging the bowl. My options were to cut another piece of stone or accept that the pipe would be imperfect. I was satisfied with the stone and continued shaping it. The work went smoothly, and EagleHeart commented that he had never seen a pipe come together so quickly.

For the stem Chris suggested using a slightly curved branch from a sumac tree. We found one on the shore of a lake nearby, and, thanking the tree for its gift to my pipe, I sawed off a limb. As we walked back to the house, I began to feel a deep tranquility within myself that I had rarely experienced.

After receiving instructions from EagleHeart, I began the laborious process of shaping the soft, warm stone into a loving peace pipe, which I did at home. The pipe was always in the back of my mind, and at work I daydreamed about how I could embellish it. Fantasizing various etched designs, but fearing a hairline crack, I heeded EagleHeart's advice. I struggled with the filing, starting with a wide-toothed file and working my way down the various grades to the fine-toothed files. Having canceled my social plans, I withdrew into the pipe making.

I began to wonder if I was I doing it the correct way. Being visually oriented, I wanted a photograph or sketch of a peace pipe, so I contacted the library. The librarian searched the system and found just one book on peace pipes. Reading from the book over the phone to me, he said that the pipes were used as a symbol of peace among North American and Canadian tribes, but peace pipes had been obsolete since the 1800's. That was strange considering that I had smoked a peace pipe a week ago at the sweat lodge.

The pipe, in its natural form, turned out beautifully, without the addition of fancy designs or patterns. The rough side flourished into a beautiful piece of work. Images emerged in the indentations: a young woman, a medicine woman elder, an eagle, a chief, a buffalo, and an Egyptian woman. It seemed that all these images were put there by the Creator millions of years ago for me to discover. My portable altar now bore strong and natural symbols that added to its supernatural quality.

I called EagleHeart to learn how to seal the pipe. He was surprised that I had finished filing and sanding; and I explained that I wanted the pipe ready for sweat lodge the following evening. There was a specialist in sealing pipes living near the Pipestone Quarry. The Quarry is in Pipestone, Minnesota, and the stone, which is used exclusively for amulets and pipes, has been quarried there for many centuries.

Only Native Americans have the right to quarry the pipestone; others can obtain the stone by purchasing it from them.

Why was I so driven to finish the pipe? I wasn't really sure. My energy was focused on its creation; it symbolized something very important to me. The pipe had waited many years to come into my life, and it was impatient.

Unconsciously protecting the pipe, I boiled and sealed it four times, wanting a good seal and a glistening sheen. It didn't turn out that way: the wax caked on the pipe, giving it a dull whitish film. There was nothing I could do about it—I had to leave for sweat lodge.

My pipe was initiated that evening, even though the stem wasn't finished. (EagleHeart lent me a stem that he had made.) Before the sweat lodge my pipe was smudged with sage to cleanse and protect it.

As I cupped the power herb's smoke in my hands and drew it around my body, I prayed for the sage's protection with humility and respect. It was one of those special events I will always remember. I felt I was graduating to a higher level of spirituality. Unbeknownst to me, EagleHeart announced to the group that I would be given an Indian Sioux name, *Canupa Lutah Winan* — Red Pipe Woman. I felt honored and slightly embarrassed at the public acknowledgement of something so personal. Because of my readings on ceremonies, I knew the naming was a painstaking procedure because of the delicate match between Mother Earth, the Great Spirit, and the spirit of the individual to be named. From that day forward, *Canupa Lutah Winan* was my given name; in the earthly and spirit world.

During the ceremony, I smudged myself thoroughly while EagleHeart used Kinnickinnick to acknowledge the four directions and Mother Earth, Father Sky, and the Great Spirit. The four directions are acknowledged because the Great Spirit uses the four winds to speak to us. At one point I held the peace pipe towards the stars while prayers were offered to the spirit world. As I chanted *Canupa Lutah Winan* to the heavens, I felt honored and blessed. Power surged through my spirit, and I experienced a deep connection between Great Spirit, my peace pipe, and my soul.

A few days after the sweat lodge, I unwrapped my pipe and inspected the waxing. It was still caked to the stone, so I tried rubbing a small area with a towel, and, to my amazement, shiny red stone peeked through the hard wax. I continued to rub furiously until all the wax had disappeared. I held my pipe in my hands and stared at it in awe. It was beautiful!

It took me a couple of weeks to come down from my sweat-lodge high. I wasn't ready to start working on the stem yet. The time just didn't feel right. I continued attending sweat lodges until a tragic event hurled me into completing the pipe.[7]

Dreams

*I dream of love and passion
deep into the night.*

*I dream of girls with fashion
I'd love to hold them tight.*

*I dream of lots of things
that I know will not come true.*

*But when my dreams are done
and I no longer dream of you*

*You will find me up in Heaven
I hope you'll be there too.*

Shane Lone Eagle

11

The Reading

July

THE CAMP ALLOWED SHANE TO VISIT ME A MONTH AFTER HIS return from the hospital. Although he was supposed to be still on medication, Shane admitted to me that he hadn't been taking it because it made his thinking fuzzy. When I teased him, calling him by his childhood nickname, "Space Trace", sadness briefly clouded over his face. He had brought his anti-depressants with him and took them sporadically, which didn't really help his mental condition at all. Anti-depressants need to be taken on a consistent basis to be effective.

This visit was different from the others because I couldn't take any time off work to be with him. Shane got bored almost immediately and asked if he could come to work with me and hang around the office. Robert, the director of the domestic abuse agency, couldn't see any harm in it. Tracy played cards with the therapists, entertained the children as they waited for their appointments with their therapists, and did odd copying and filing jobs around the office.

On the weekend we planned on having his friend Tricia over for dinner. Shane picked out the food he wanted me to prepare: spaghetti, bread, and cake. I insisted on a vegetable, so he chose salad. We went shopping together and cleaned the condo, both excited about our visitor. Actually Shane was as skittish as a cat, wandering around mumbling about whether we had enough food, or if she'd even like the dinner.

"And don't do anything weird to the food," he warned me. I knew he was thinking of the time he had wanted shrimp for dinner, and I had broiled them. Disgusted by the way the shrimp looked—all red and veined—Shane insisted that it wasn't shrimp because it didn't have a covering over it; everyone knew that shrimp was brown. Of course he meant battered shrimp. Another time he'd wanted a grilled cheese sandwich, but refused to eat the one I made, swearing that I was trying to poison him with bad cheese. I had used white cheese instead of yellow, and Shane thought it was old and spoiled.

The funniest time was when Shane and I had lunch at Red Lobster with Robert. We ordered our entrees while the waitress brought us a basket containing four long, slender, beige-colored tubes—freshly baked bread sticks— salted and dripping with butter. Robert and I grabbed one each and began gnawing on them. Shane curled up his lip and asked what the gross thing in the basket was.

I calmly replied, "Octopus Legs," and carried on chewing.

Robert, catching on, said "Yea, Shane, try one. The barnacles are great!"

Shane was so disgusted that he ran out of the dining room, frantically searching for the bathroom. Robert and I howled with laughter.

Dinner was excellent, or, more accurately, I should say that Tricia and I enjoyed our dinner. Shane picked at his food and complained throughout the meal. Tricia and I couldn't help looking at each other and giggling, but Shane caught us in the act, so we held back. I washed the dishes while they played computer games, and it was soon time to take Tricia home.

I waited in the car as Shane walked her to the door. Once again, that weird yet familiar feeling came over me. It's hard to describe it. I felt overwhelmed by responsibility, knowing that Shane depended on me so heavily, and helpless because I couldn't help him the way I wanted. At least I was past the point of questioning whether I was acting the appropriate way. I easily slipped into the role of being an older sister, but that didn't help Shane. He needed guidance and an authority figure who could nurture him. A year ago I felt like a teenager dressed up in adult clothes, pretending to be a mother. I no longer feel that insecurity, what was left was uncertainty of his future.

This visit was a struggle for me. Shane was still deeply depressed and unable to feel satisfied with anything or enjoy the time we had together. I was very concerned about him and entertained the idea of his living with me again. This time I wouldn't include Krissy in the arrangement, but would move out of my condo and find a home large enough for both of us. Krissy had little contact with Shane after he returned to the reservation, and I was disappointed in her. I had hoped she would have maintained some communication with Shane, respecting his need for consistency in his life. I suspected that Shane, who never mentioned her, thought that Krissy deserted him because he ran away from her home. I didn't mention my idea to Shane, but sent a letter to Steve at the Camp, informing him that I was interested in providing foster care for Shane. I never received a response and didn't pursue it, thinking that perhaps the Camp had other plans for him.

That summer Shane broke both his arms, although not at the same time. He broke his right arm playing HackySak, and the left arm a couple weeks later when he tried to catch himself as he fell off a horse. Both his arms were in casts, but they didn't heal properly because Shane kept breaking off the casts. Time after time, I lectured him that his bones had to heal completely, but he complained about his restricted movement and his arms being itchy. I didn't understand where he was coming from until I came across a description from a pamphlet at a trading post store on his reservation: *"Being Indian is . . . cutting off your cast after two weeks because it's in the way and isn't needed anyway."* [1]

A truly life-threatening event also occurred that same summer for Shane. He had an allergic reaction to a horsefly bite. Luckily Donald, Shane's roommate, noticed his severe reaction to the bite and notified their house parent, saying that Shane was probably experiencing an allergic reaction. They carried Shane into a car and started out for the hospital. About halfway there, Shane lost consciousness and stopped breathing. Donald performed mouth-to-mouth resuscitation on him until Shane began breathing on his own. Shane stopped breathing three more times before they reached the hospital, and each time Donald managed to revive him.

When they arrived at the hospital Shane was given an antidote, which brought him fully conscious and alert within thirty minutes. According to the emergency room staff, Donald had saved Shane's life. He later received an award from the JD Camp.

Meanwhile, I had been sailing in the Apostle Islands of northern Wisconsin and had no idea anything was wrong until I got home. Shane called me from the hospital, complaining in a raspy voice that he wasn't getting any visitors and was bored. I tried to explain to him that there was no way I could take additional time off to drive to North Dakota, but I could tell he was disappointed and wanted me there. I tried to comfort him over the telephone, but he wouldn't have it. They kept him at the hospital under observation for a few days before releasing him with a clean bill of health. I felt extremely guilty but justified my actions by rationalizing that he had plenty of people around him. My absence wouldn't have much of an impact on him.

Each year, towards the end of summer, the Renaissance Fair was on the prairie lands surrounding the Twin Cities. Held in August, the heat and humidity was suffocating. The ground cover dust is so thick that all the fairgoers were covered with a gritty film by the time they have walked from their cars to the entrance gate. In spite of these minor discomforts, it's a very popular event—a combination celebration and farewell to summer.

Actors in period costumes play character roles; performances are delivered throughout the day. Sporting events such as jousting and wrestling are held, and there is a sprinkling of arts and crafts. It was an event I looked forward to.

That day tarot readings were being offered at a few small tables under the cool shade of a large oak tree. My friend Joyce and I strolled towards their direction. Joyce chose a middle-aged man with an interesting face to give her a general reading while I waited at a picnic table. She came back elated with promises of a new job, a special relationship, and improved finances.

I went to the same reader, hoping to be told of good health and a long-lasting relationship with James. As I sat at the table, the reader shuffled the cards and laid them out in a pattern. I began to sense some discomfort in him as he stared at the cards at length. Shaking his head, he scooped up the spread and reshuffled the deck. He laid the cards out in a different pattern, and again stared at them. This time he raised his eyes to mine, then lowered them again to the cards.

"Has anyone close to you been ill?" he quietly questioned me. I thought for a while, but didn't have any friends or family who were ill.

"It looks like a male," he pursued.

Shaking my head, I started to feel angry. What kind of reading was this? I considered asking for my money back.

He leaned close and whispered, "Someone—a male—who is very close to you will die."

I jumped back, unable to reply.

He continued, "I usually don't read the cards this way, but the message came up in both spreads, so I had to tell you."

Speechless, I nodded, pushed my chair back and walked quickly over to Joyce. Assuming that my reading had been just as wonderful as hers, she wanted to compare notes and speculate on her future good fortune. I put her off saying, "It was okay, but I really don't believe in that stuff anyway."

Seeming at a loss for words, Joyce suggested we get something to eat at one of the booths.

I was unusually quiet for the rest of the afternoon as I dwelled on the possibility that James might die. For some reason, I was sure it wasn't my father or any of my uncles or other male friends. No, I was certain it had to be James. I drove home planning to enjoy the short time I had left with James and promising myself never to tell him about the reading.

Joyce was more intuitive than I had anticipated, and she called me the next day asking if I was angry with her. After briefly debating with myself whether to tell her about the reading, I decided that I needed some advice. After listening to my story, she insisted on my telling James, if for no other reason than to dissipate some of the energy I had built up around the reading.

"Our strong expectations can sometimes make things happen, and you don't want that, do you?" she asked earnestly.

So I called James and sheepishly described the reading and my interpretation of it. He listened quietly and assured me that he didn't have an illness or a death wish. I tried to explain how important he was to me and how unbearable it would be to lose him. Our conversation brought us closer together—sharing my innermost feelings strengthened our bond. Maybe this was the intention of the reading, I mused. Things are not always as they seem.

This deeper intimacy that we were experiencing led us to talk about how wonderful it would be to take a long trip together. We decided we'd like to drive down to Mexico for a month or two, then travel back through the Southwest, up the West Coast, and into Canada. We wouldn't return to Minnesota, both dreading the severe winters, and speculated where we might settle down for permanent residence.

We planned to quit our jobs as we'd be traveling for a year or more. We began to get organized; selling my car, buying a trailer that we'd live in while we traveled, and wrapping up loose ends at our jobs. I had always wanted to travel like this—feeling free to go wherever and do whatever I wanted, and the timing couldn't have been better. I was feeling burned out in my career. The horrific stories I heard every day in counseling sessions were beginning to merge into each other, sounding repetitive and mundane. I needed a fresh perspective, time to purge my mind and body of the trauma I had been working with for the past few years, and a chance to learn of my next step in life. I was so excited planning my new life that I was almost able to ignore a tiny inner voice asking me how Shane would handle this. I ignored it.

Life had a way of sneaking up on me; that old saying "We plan, God laughs" was so true in my life. Within a month, Shane called me, late one evening. He was attending the wake of his mother. Marlina died alone in Seattle, Washington. She had cirrhosis of the liver and died an excruciating death. Her body had been flown back to the reservation. For the first time in many years she had actually been welcomed by her people.

Shane explained that her funeral would last for two days—the time it took for the spirit to leave the body. He emphasized that the family had to stay awake the entire night with his mother's body to ward off bad spirits and help lead his mother to the other world.

Suddenly I heard kids screaming and laughing in the background, and Shane, in a rush, told me he had to go and hung up. I felt disconnected, lost between my comfortable little world and Shane's. I wanted to be in Shane's world, to support him and his sisters while they said their goodbyes to Marlina. I sat in the dark for a long time, my mind wandering among bits and pieces of memories.

Knowing Shane wouldn't be able to answer my questions about Sioux belief in death and dying, I met with EagleHeart and tried to make sense of Marlina's death. She had been thirty-three years old and alienated from all five of her children (two from another relationship lived with their paternal grandmother). I had wanted some kind of reconciliation between Marlina and the children, but she died leaving them without peace or tranquility. I don't remember any specific phrase or answer from EagleHeart, but my head cleared, and I left feeling some comfort.

I admit that I had contempt for Marlina. I suffered the results of her abusive punishment towards Shane. It was fairly simple for me to place her in the "Bad Guy" position, while I offered the safe haven for her son. When dealing with physical and psychological abuse it's so much easier to look at the dynamics in black and white, good guy / bad guy mentality. The victim is the good guy, while the abuser is the bad guy. Marlina fit the bad guy role perfectly, and I fit the good guy...maybe not so perfectly. But was she really the bad mother? Or was she sick, wrought with alcoholism and drug abuse, living in an environment that aged her beyond her years, struggling to have a relationship with her children?

Even as I tried to think about this, I answered back in defense of the children, screaming out her faults and errors in judgment. Maybe this principle is so difficult to apply because it is the wrong principle. What do I know of this woman? Yes, she threatened my life a few times, severely damaged her children through neglect, but is she bad?

I'd like her to fulfill that role. It would have made things a lot simpler for me to understand and place blame. But Shane was a part of her, and Allana and Missy are her blood. If I hate Marlina I then hate Shane's sisters, and I cannot hate them. This is the struggle I lived with.

Psychological studies on suicidal adolescents revealed that family factors increased Shane's suicide risk; including loss of a family member and feeling ignored by parents or caregivers. In a study published by the Canadian Journal of Psychiatry, 1994[2], suicidal adolescents identified specific triggers called acute stressors. Those affecting Shane included death of a loved one, a major change in his teenage years, chronic strain of alcohol problems in his family, dating stress, and school stress. His suicide risk was blown off the map.

That suicidology theory was six years into the future, and it was just a matter of time before I had to tell Shane I was moving away from him. I found myself postponing the inevitable. Oh, yes, I felt guilty. What timing on my part; first he loses his mother, then he loses his anchor to the white world. But my feelings of guilt wouldn't help either of us. I had to go on the trip for my own growth, and Shane had to get on with his life. He was almost seventeen years old now—a young man.

12

Dark Side of the Soul

October

I WANTED TO ATTEND AS MANY SWEAT LODGES AS I COULD before our trip, which was about two months away; so, on the night of the October full moon I participated in a sweat lodge that was exclusively for women.

Entering the lodge I felt ambivalent, which was unusual. I usually felt peaceful as the darkness blanketed me. As I circled clockwise around the fire pit I began to feel extremely anxious. Trying to calm myself, I prayed to the Great Spirit for strength to endure this night. I made it through the first endurance, but the second endurance was horrible. The heat made my breathing strained and heavy, and the walls seemed to be closing in on me, making me claustrophobic. I felt a cold wind blowing over my right shoulder and shivered, even though I was sweating profusely.

During the third endurance, this wind moved over my head and whirled above me. Suddenly the lodge became suffocatingly hot and I began to hyperventilate. I tried to concentrate on the prayers going on, but I was pulled by the wind hovering above me. I was frightened and my heart throbbed wildly. The wind brushed my hair and the claws of a gigantic bird dug into my scalp, grabbing my hair. I questioned the bird, asking the aberration what it wanted. A beautiful, powerful eagle flew in front of me, commanding me to fly with it, to join it on a journey. Instantly I was lifted up by its clenched claws and carried above the lodge, the city, and Minnesota.

As we flew above snow-capped mountains and turquoise seas, the eagle tucked me under its downy wing and asked me to join him in the spirit world. I was tempted, but knew it wasn't appropriate for me to go with the eagle. The second I hesitated I was jolted back into my body. He fluttered above me while I explained that I wasn't ready and why I was afraid to go with him. The eagle gave an ear-piercing shriek and disappeared.

The fourth endurance seemed to last just a few seconds. I was consumed with intense sadness and confusion. I left the sweat lodge feeling deep, consuming grief. I tried to tell myself that I was just tired and a good night's sleep would ease my feelings, but I was wrong. After a fitful night, I awoke feeling overwhelmed by sadness and emptiness, and barely made it through the day without bursting into uncontrollable tears. It was true that I'd been under a great amount of stress, planning the trip and putting an end to my career, but this didn't feel like an appropriate reaction to stress.

I preoccupied myself with the details of moving and attributed my drastic mood changes, especially the deep sadness, to leaving family and friends. In fact I was so preoccupied that I almost forgot Shane's seventeenth birthday. It was in the back of my mind, but I kept forgetting to get him a present.

I managed to reach him at the JD Camp the evening of his birthday, and realized as I did so that I hadn't heard from him for a few weeks. He was somewhat distant on the phone, and I apologized for not having his gift there on his birthday, but suggested coming to visit him and bringing the gift with me. He made excuses, saying that he was busy, he wouldn't have time to see me, and I didn't have to visit him. Feeling very guilty, I tried to push the issue, but Shane seemed to be in a hurry to get off the phone. Even though the timing wasn't the best, I knew I had to begin preparing him for my departure in two months. I described the upcoming trip and promised that I'd keep in contact with him. He didn't have much to say and quickly ended the conversation.

Thursday, October 7th

Two days later, around 9:00 p.m., I received a phone call from Shane's counselor at the JD Camp in Williston. He told me that, earlier that evening, Shane had taken his own life. As I listened, an image of a fist the size of a basketball, shielded with black thick iron, loomed six feet in front of me. Stunned, I watched the fist charge into my stomach, enter my solar plexus, and grab my insides. Moaning, I doubled over in pain. The dark fist withdrew; my guts, dripping blood, in its grip. The pain disappeared but a hole remained inside my stomach. Black and empty.

Still on the phone, Steve was yelling, "Are you there? Are you okay?" I couldn't answer him, I was gasping for breath. He began to panic and asked if I was alone in the house. A distant part of me realized that he was screening me for suicide potential, so I slowly replied that my father was in the other room. Sensing that I was safe, he told me the funeral would be on Monday at Shane's reservation.

"How did he kill himself?" I managed to whisper.

"He hung himself in his closet after supper. We didn't find his body for several hours." After checking to make sure Shane's sisters had been notified, I hung up the phone.

James and my dad sat up with me until dawn, when I finally collapsed with exhaustion. As I began to drift into a restless sleep, I glanced at the dresser and saw my pipe. It was time.

A few hours later I picked up the pipe, and a small piece of bead work fell to the floor. I stared at it and remembered how Shane had showed off his masterpiece to me. The bead work had won first prize at the Pow Wow held on his reservation every summer. He also had danced as one of the Fancy Dancers for a few years when he was younger but lost interest as the city life became his priority. He had been so proud of the bead work, and even though I wasn't an impartial judge, I thought the workmanship was excellent. He had forgotten to take it with him, and I had wondered for weeks if he would let me use it on the yet-to-be-completed pipe stem. I had put off calling him, trying to be honest with myself that my intentions were honorable. When I finally managed to ask him, Shane had thought it was a great idea.

I picked up the dried Sumac branch that I would use for the stem and began stripping off the bark with a filet knife. Five layers of wood—green, blonde, brown, white, and black—were swiftly discarded before I had the basic shape I wanted.

Four hours later, the stem was fairly smooth but still needed sanding, which I did for the rest of the evening. Friends came over to express their sadness at Shane's death. Several of them wanted to attend the funeral but didn't have the time to travel the 300 miles to get there. One actually asked if I would be willing to have a service here for Shane. How could I endure two funerals? I didn't think I could make it through one. She asked me to think about it while I was in North Dakota.

On Saturday I picked up blonde calfskin for the pipe bag. This may sound like an easy thing to do, but I was in such a state of shock that making the smallest decision seemed beyond me. I finally chose a bolt of leather and asked for a couple of yards.

"Sorry," said the clerk, "you have to buy the entire hide."

At eight dollars a yard, it would have cost over a hundred dollars, and I certainly didn't need a whole hide. I rummaged through a remnant bin and dug out a piece with a few defects.

Glancing at the speedometer as I drove back to the house, I saw that I was going fifty miles an hour in a thirty-mile zone. My foot was on the gas pedal, but I didn't have any control over it. I tried to lift my foot off the pedal, but it was frozen. I heard Shane's voice echo through the car, "Hey Deb, why didn't you let me drive? This is fun!"

I gripped the wheel so hard my fingers turned white, shook my head, and tried to clear my thoughts. I regained control of the accelerator and cautiously drove the rest of the way at a snail's pace. Friends chauffeured me around for a while after that experience.

Staring at the leather laid out on the kitchen table, I wondered how I was going to make a pipe bag. I had never seen one. I laid the stem and pipe next to each other and cut out a semblance of a pattern. Using a leather punch, I made lacing holes around the circumference, leaving the top open for a drawstring. Later, EagleHeart had told me that the pipe turns into a sacred object once it is connected to the stem; therefore the pipe bag had to hold the pipe and stem separately. Saturday afternoon, the bag was done.

I'm sure my family and close friends thought I had lost my mind, or was in shock about Shane's death. I was chasing around finishing a pipe when I should have been mourning in a more appropriate manner. I was driven. No, that isn't a strong enough word. I was overpowered by a force much stronger than myself to complete it, and in my state of mind I responded without questioning. After the iron fist incident I knew there were spiritual powers controlling the situation. I complied with their wishes.

13

Wrathful Eagle

AT HALF PAST SIX ON SUNDAY MORNING, JAMES, MY SISTER Tara, and I set out for the ten-hour drive. We followed the familiar road I had traveled so many times; only this time Shane wouldn't be waiting at the other end. The road stretched on and on, and each hour seemed like four. I suppose I was experiencing some of the stages of grief: one minute afraid and wanting to turn back, the next minute convincing myself that Shane was alive, and we were being ridiculous for getting so upset over nothing. Pretending Shane was alive was a good coping skill, and I subconsciously clung to this belief until I actually saw his body.

We arrived at Cammie's home—the girls' foster mother—around supper time. Allana and Missy took us out for a walk to show Tara the beautiful hills and valleys. This was Tara's first time on the Reservation. The wake was the next afternoon, and we spent a quiet evening talking with the girls about their mother's death and funerals in general. Allana repeatedly warned me that Shane's funeral would last throughout the night with numerous services. As she talked, I began to feel anxious and looked towards James for support. In ten hours I would know the truth. Please let it be someone else who had died, I silently pleaded.

Monday was a beautiful, warm fall day. The sun shone brilliantly, and billowy clouds floated across a vivid blue sky. We forced ourselves to eat some breakfast and then began our search for star blankets. Sioux tradition dictated that six five-pointed-star blankets hung behind the casket, Allana informed us. Each star represents a spirit. The colors on the blanket represents Father Sky, Mother Earth, and the four directions. Shane's Uncle Leonard told her the blankets would be at the bingo hall (which also served as a gym and funeral home).

We searched, but there were no blankets anywhere in the bingo hall. In fact, it still had decorations up from the previous night's bingo game. Allana was becoming distraught, close to losing control. I sympathized with her, knowing I wouldn't have been coping as well as she was at fifteen years old, having lost both her mother and older brother within weeks of each other.

I put my own feelings of loss aside and pounced into action. Trying to console her, I said, "We'll just go to your relatives and get all the blankets we need."

She stared at me with blank eyes and answered, "No, we just won't have the blankets." I countered her, insisting that there had to be a number of people with star blankets covering their beds.

Allana revived a little and exclaimed, "The priest lives right next door, and he has one. I know he does. I saw it. And my uncle lives down the street. He'll know who has the blankets!"

"Let's get a move on then," Tara yelled, and pushed us out of the hall.

Allana ran ahead of us and knocked on the door of the rectory. After what seemed like ages, a young man, dressed in jeans and a t-shirt, whom I assumed to be the priest answered. Allana stepped away from the door, waiting expectantly for me to explain our predicament. I stumbled for words but couldn't speak, so James stepped forward and asked the priest for a star blanket. Suspicious, the priest looked at each of us in turn. We evidently passed inspection because he told us to come back in an hour or so. He didn't acknowledge that he had a blanket, however.

"Okay," my sister said, "where does this Uncle Leonard live?"

Allana led us down a dirt bike path. The houses were prefabricated from the early seventies, but obviously well maintained. Flowers and shrubs were planted in the yards, and it resembled a white middle-class suburb. I hadn't met any of the relatives, so Allana filled me in on Uncle Leonard's connection to Shane. He was her mother's brother and had helped organize Marlina's funeral. Naively, I assumed he would organize Shane's funeral, especially once he met us and became aware of Allana's state of mind. Shane had no close family other than his sisters, and Allana couldn't be expected to handle her brother's funeral.

Uncle Leonard answered the door, glaring at all of us. I could see the unspoken thought in his eyes, 'Who are you and why did Allana bring you to my home?'

After a brief introduction, he asked us to come in, and we sat at the kitchen table with great trepidation. I have never felt so much anxiety about blankets! Allana explained her predicament. Ignoring her plea, Uncle Leonard instead inquired about her arrangements for the grave digger. I was astonished. He really expected a fifteen year old to arrange this? Allana stumbled over her words, glancing over at me, and finally replied, "I hadn't thought about it."

"Well you'd better. Where did you think they'd put the casket? Here," he said, handing her the phone, "call up Joe and ask him if he can dig the grave tomorrow morning. The funeral is tomorrow afternoon, so you'd better get moving."

I sat at the table biting my tongue. I couldn't say a word. I was white, a stranger in his home. I had no right to interfere. Allana stared at me with wide eyes, beseeching me for help. Silently, I told her I couldn't help her; she had to do it alone. After a few long seconds, she sighed deeply and dialed the number. Stumbling over the words, she spoke to the grave digger and made the arrangements. Uncle Leonard then promised he'd get three blankets, but told Allana she had to get the others. Each of us profusely thanked him and made a very quick exit.

Breathing a long sigh of relief, I asked, "What next?"

James pointed to the rectory, and there we picked up blanket number four. Two more to go. Having an actual blanket in hand put us in a better mood. It seemed as if we were trying to pass some sick right of passage. As we walked down the steps towards the car, I saw a black and white feather lying in the freshly mown grass. It became my first peace pipe feather. I had brought the pipe with me, but EagleHeart recommended that I not flash it around or offer to do ceremonies with it. Some tribal members wouldn't welcome a woman pipe carrier, he warned. I appreciated his warning, but that was the last thing I wanted to do, it was more a source of comfort and strength for me.

After a few hours we succeeded in rounding up all the blankets through the priest's generous intervention. We carefully hung the blankets in a specific pattern while others arranged the hall for a funeral. Within an hour the hall looked very sedate, and at noon I prepared myself to meet the hearse that carried Shane's body.

The hearse stopped five miles away from the reservation boundaries to allow family members and friends to escort the body onto the reservation. Four cars, packed to the fenders with elders, adolescents, adults, babies, and school children awaited the arrival. Still convinced that there had been a mistake, I minimized the situation. Some other poor child had died, I told myself, it wasn't Shane. I felt sad for the parents of the other child, but was secretly relieved it wasn't him. We followed the hearse to the hall, and four men carried the casket inside, setting it in front of the blankets alongside the flower arrangements.

People bustled around nervously, arranging and rearranging chairs. Women were in the kitchen chopping vegetables and making soup. Through the commotion, I heard a thumping coming from the ceiling. It sounded as if someone was walking rapidly back and forth on the roof. Assuming someone was patching the roof shingles, I ignored it.

The priest entered the hall and went directly to the casket, ignoring greetings and small talk. He stood facing the casket, and immediately people sat down and a hush fell over the room. I sat a few feet in front of the casket with James and Tara on my right and Shane's sisters hovering over my shoulders. As the priest began his prayers, Missy stormed out of the hall, running as if her life depended on it. I began to rise to follow her, but James gently took my hand, shaking his head. I knew if I ran after her I would miss seeing the casket's lid raised, and I could postpone the inevitable a little bit longer.

As the priest turned and began to lift the lid, I heard Uncle Leonard screaming. The priest ignored the commotion and continued praying.

I turned my head away, but my morbid curiosity overtook me and I stared at the face. My mind silently screamed, "NO, OH MY GOD!" as I saw the child lying in cold metal, the child who had become a part of my being and soul. The room dimmed, then darkened and my body melted into the chair. As James put his arm around my shoulders, the lights began to brighten and the casket came into focus again. I couldn't stare at the body for longer than a few seconds without feeling faint, so I concentrated on my shoelaces, glancing up when the feeling passed.

Allana rushed up to Shane, touching his arm and stroking his hair with her fingers. I tried to follow but began to feel nauseated as I neared the body. I sat back down and watched as Allana asked James to take photographs of her standing with Shane. Shane's nine year old half sister Verna, who lived with her paternal grandmother, stood next to Allana and James took cameo and portrait shots. This was so strange for me; I was raised Catholic and was taught never to touch the body or take photographs. I had to restrain myself from rushing up to the children and scolding them for being so sacrilegious. As no other adults were aghast at their behavior, I gathered that this was normal in their culture. Allana called me over for a photo with her and Shane, but I declined.

Shane looked so different. He was dressed in a borrowed suit, with a black bow tie covering his neck. His face was swollen and the skin below his lower lip was white. The skin coloring was all wrong; he looked as if he'd slapped on instant tanning lotion; that sickening orange tint was on his face, ears, and hands. It was Shane's body, yet it wasn't him.

Someone led me over to the food table and James filled a plate for both of us. I forced myself to eat a little because I didn't want to insult the cooks, but I had a hard time swallowing anything. I looked around to see how the girls were coping. Allana entered the hall, leading Missy towards our table. Missy had run out to their mother's grave and had fallen asleep by the headstone. Both were hungry, but Allana insisted that Missy have her photo taken next to Shane before they ate.

After an hour or so, the visitors who had come to offer their condolences left, and Allana explained what would happen for the next twenty-four hours. The family members were required to stay the entire night, assisting and guiding the spirit into the next world. She wasn't exactly clear about how we were to do this, only that we had to be present. The priest would arrive in the evening, around half past seven, for the wake and rosary service, and food would be served after the service. Female elders would be praying Sioux songs and chants, again to guide the spirit, and this would continue until sunrise. Explaining that this was the only free time we'd have to shower and change, Allana suggested we should drive back to Cammie's house and prepare for an overnighter at the bingo hall.

James, Tara, and I, along with Missy, Allana, and Verna went into Wanagi Lake for pizza before making our way back to the hall. Away from the reservation, we laughed and joked, partly to break up the somber mood that seemed to permeate the reservation. Allana and Verna told us that Shane had left a suicide note for one of his girlfriends, but the police hadn't released it yet. They had heard there was another note, but it wasn't clear who the note was addressed to. We speculated about what Shane had written and who the mystery person could be, but all too soon we had to return to the reality of the funeral.

The room was about half full, with children running around, tripping and falling over one another, and adults calming their nerves by chain smoking. I didn't know the majority of the people, but James, Tara, and I were the only strangers in the room. There were other white people there, but it was obvious they were known to the community. People stared at us and pointed, but Allana and Missy kept us busy, introducing us to their friends.

People began taking their seats and settling down as a procession of priests entered the hall, with the pacing sound from the roof echoing throughout the hall. The oldest priest sprinkled holy water on the casket as he mumbled some prayers, then began to address us in a stern, authoritative voice, admonishing all of us for the delinquency of the teenagers. He wrathfully denounced television as a major contributor to the degeneration of teenage morals; the allegedly free-flowing sexual activity as a leading cause of world corruption; and he demanded that the teenagers in attendance listen and obey their parents, implying that they would end up like Shane if they didn't.

I was horrified! It was the most insulting sermon I had ever heard, and totally inappropriate for the situation. Wondering if this was a typical sermon from this priest, I looked at the faces of the people around me; some were sleeping, others fastidiously picked lint from their sweaters, and the teens were spacing out, gazing at the bright spotlights on the ceiling.

His sermon didn't end a minute too soon for me—he harassed us for about forty-five minutes. At least half the people rushed out of the building as soon as he had finished, as if abandoning a sinking ship, mumbling their goodbyes as they raced to their cars. The other half stayed to mingle, drink coffee and smoke some more. Men passed around baskets brimming with cigarettes, and, by the time the baskets had reached the back of the room, they were empty. The teens were running wild outside, screaming and wrestling with each other, gathering in the dark recesses of the parking lot. The priest had left the crowd in a very agitated state, and I wondered if fights ever broke out at these wakes.

As the evening wore on, the teenagers' hyperactivity increased with the temperature in the room. It was as if we were in an oven whose heat was steadily rising. The parents ignored the commotion, talking among themselves and getting up periodically to refill their coffee cups. And the pacing on the roof would sporadically echo throughout the room, then disappear. Someone murmured that Shane's spirit was restless, awaiting the guidance into the spirit world. A group of female elders continued their wail of grief every twenty minutes or so, the sound blending in with the growing pandemonium.

A flurry of new activity at the west door of the hall caught my attention. A tall man in his forties, glancing nervously through the gathering crowd, caught my eye but quickly glanced away. Not looking at the casket, he walked straight to the back of the room and stood alone, watching those who were watching him. I was one of the watchers, or, I should say, I was staring rudely at him. His profile resembled Shane's, and as he stared at me, he nodded. This was Shane's father.

His father and family never acknowledged Shane as his son, and in fact, adamantly denied it up to this day. What the reasons were, only Shane's father and mother knew. Shane's father refused to participate in the funeral plans, even though he had been called upon by several Tribal Council members. This was a powerful message to the community, stating, in public, that Shane was indeed his son.

My feelings were numb. Intense emotions were buried and the tears that I needed to shed were nonexistent. I was grateful that I wasn't crying for I feared once I started it would be weeks before I regained control. I also couldn't afford to be emotional around the girls; they needed my strength, and I was willing to give as much as they wanted. Unfortunately, the tears did come. Krissy walked into the bingo hall at the precise moment I was staring at the entrance door. Our eyes met and I broke out in heart-wrenching sobs so loudly people around me were startled. I ran to her and hugged her as I wept. In the shock of Shane's death, I had completely forgotten to contact Krissy, so it was a complete surprise to see her. Feeling guilty that I hadn't notified her, I tried to explain myself but she waved it away, and greeted Missy and Allana.

People quickly grew bored with the newcomers and went back to socializing. Tara, Krissy, and I were talking when a teenage girl rushed up to us, screaming that Missy had fainted and turned blue. We ran out of the hall, up the hill, and found Missy sprawled on the grass. Her breathing was shallow and she didn't respond when we called her name. We slapped her across the face, hoping to wake her up, but she didn't move. I asked what had happened, and one of the kids told me that she'd done this before. She had spells and was sometimes unconscious for twenty minutes or so. As we rubbed her hands and feet and called her name, she began to shake violently.

Tara and I carried her into the hall, calling out to the kids to phone for an ambulance. Someone pushed tables together and we laid her on her back. Blankets were tossed on her, but her body temperature seemed to be dropping rapidly because her face and lips were blue. A crowd gathered around us with people pushing, trying to see what was going on. Her breathing was inconsistent. She would stop breathing for a few seconds, and, only after we repeatedly screamed "Breathe" at her, would she begin to take shallow breaths.

As Tara continued to monitor her, I felt myself rise above Missy, and saw Marlina calling her towards the spirit world. Shane was gone, and a part of Missy wanted to die. As her mother continued to pull her, Missy's spirit body looked at me and said, "I don't want to die."

I quickly returned to normal consciousness, and saw that Missy was fading away. Chanting her name over and over, in a clear, calm, commanding voice, I worked at pulling her spirit back into her body. Just as I began to think it wasn't going to work, she moved, took a few breaths, then began to hyperventilate. Someone pushed a paper bag towards us and yelled that we should make her breathe into it. Her eyes were still closed and her skin was a grayish color.

I continued saying her name and stroking her hair. As soon as I stopped talking, her body started to shake, and she lapsed into unconsciousness. I yelled at her, "You cannot die. Your sister needs you. Don't let yourself die!"

People were looking at me with puzzled expressions, and someone gently touched my shoulder, speaking to me as if I were a child, "She gets these spells all the time. She won't die, just has to sleep it off. She's had this ever since her mother died."

Well, that was all I needed to hear. I continued to work on her with even more determination and could feel Missy clinging onto every word I said. I also felt her ambivalence as she struggled to choose which reality she wanted.

As the wail of the approaching siren increased, Missy gasped for air, her chest heaving with the struggle. By the time the paramedics arrived, she was breathing more consistently. James stayed close by my side as they put her in the ambulance, hooked her up to oxygen, and set off for the hospital, which was twenty minutes away.

Later, James told me how some of the others had reacted to Missy's spell. A few women tried to minimize the seriousness of it, commenting that it was an attention-getting strategy, and I was feeding right into it. Some wondered why the kids got themselves so worked up. The elders were chanting Oglala prayers for spirit cleansing and helping Shane's spirit be at rest, perceiving that the incident had a connection to the spirit world. One person had cried out, "These poor, poor kids." James had caught himself holding his breath, subconsciously trying to give his oxygen to Missy.

A small group of us—teenagers and adults—piled into cars to follow the ambulance. Verna rode with us, sitting on my lap. In the midst of our small talk, she told me in a sweet voice that she experienced the same spells as her sister, only her's lasted longer. I asked her when these spells had started, and she casually replied, "Right after my mom died."

Was she telling stories and trying to get attention? Who knows. I was too exhausted to even react.

After several hours at the hospital, Missy was sedated, told to go home and sleep, and released. The doctor had no explanation for her body's reaction. His only advice was to make an appointment with her family physician. As soon as we got back to the reservation, Missy took off with her friends and went cruising for a couple of hours while we returned to the hall.

Most of the people had left, which wasn't surprising since it was half past two in the morning. I convinced James and Tara to go and get some sleep, explaining that I needed them to be strong for the funeral. A few women remained in the kitchen; the chanting women were still in the main hall; and one woman was sitting alone, eyes closed, mouth moving silently.

I needed some air, so I took a walk around the building. About fifty feet ahead of me in the dark, I could hear drums and chanting. I couldn't see anyone but felt a stirring around me. I didn't want to be out there. I was scared and didn't want to see something I wasn't supposed to, the traditional ways were scorned upon by many of the people living on the reservation. I hurried back inside. The girls were waiting for me, and we pushed a few long banquet tables together to make our beds. I curled up in my coat and tried to sleep on the cold, hard surface. The hall lights blazed through my eyelids, and my back spasmed. My muscles had been tense the entire day, my adrenaline still pumped, and I couldn't relax enough to fall asleep. I tossed and turned, listening to the footsteps on the roof. It seemed that Shane couldn't sleep either . . .

At about half past seven in the morning James and Tara returned and took me to Cammie's. As I quickly showered and changed clothes for ten o'clock Mass, James described what had happened the night before on their drive back to Cammie's. In a pool of blood in the middle of the highway they had seen the severed head of a three-point buck. There were no other cars on the road, no houses in the distance, only the head, facing north, with its eyes wide open, as if in terror. Someone had dragged the head into the center of the road and left it for others to find. Thinking it was a prank, James slowed the car, but as he got closer to the head, it simply evaporated. Worried that he was hallucinating from exhaustion, he asked Tara if she had seen anything. In a shaky, questioning voice, she said she thought she had. They drove the rest of the way cautiously and in silence, unwilling to discuss it further until they had had some sleep.

I wasn't surprised when I heard about it. With everything else that was happening, nothing seemed strange. We seemed to be caught up in a surrealistic dream.

As we drove back to the hall, I noticed that the weather was unusually warm, bright and sunny, with a strong north wind. The north represents purification, cleansing, wisdom and knowledge. I prayed for stamina. It was going to be another very long day.

The hall buzzed with activity as we entered. People stood in a long line in front of the casket, saying their final farewells to Shane. I watched the procession with little emotion, knowing that his spirit wasn't in his body. It was above the building, as the footsteps had confirmed. Four pallbearers from the JD Camp carried the casket across the school yard to the small chapel. We followed, surrounded by the sounds of grief. My defenses began to finally break and I began weeping softly, my energy and strength depleted. James put his arm around my waist and escorted me up the chapel steps. I sat in the second pew with James at my side. I had difficulty controlling my sobs and tried to stifle them.

As the organ music began, the priest and altar boys walked down the aisle to the altar. I immediately recognized the priest and assured myself that he wouldn't preach the same sermon twice.

He began his tirade about parents and teenagers who sin, and he included sex, VCRs, and playing bingo among his list. James nudged me and pointed to his eyes. Looking around I saw that everyone was dry-eyed. I too had stopped crying and was getting angry all over again, thinking that the priest had some nerve talking about these things at a funeral service. My attention drifted, and I imagined Shane opening the casket, sitting up and laughing, "Hey, you guys, what're you doing? It's just a joke."

When it was time for communion, the priest made an announcement: "I know some people are here who do not belong to the faith. I hope those who worship heathen gods will redeem themselves and come to the flock. You know who you are, and you cannot partake in the communion of the Lord."

'I'm Catholic and wouldn't accept communion from you in a million years', I thought to myself. Several unrecognizable organ pieces echoed in the background as the communion line wore on. I supposed some individuals didn't feel as insulted as I did. My mind drifted and I started to prepare myself for the burial. Then I heard a tune that was unmistakable. Chills ran down my spine, and my palms started to perspire, and I tried to hold back my tears. It was *The Rose*[1].

"*Some say love is like a hunger, an endless, aching need . . .* " I thought of Shane's hunger; his love for his mother that was never satisfied; his constant searching for her, always hoping she would give her love to him.

" *. . . love, it is a razor, it leads your soul to bleed . . .* " I saw Shane's troubled face as he was rejected again by his mother. I heard the sadness and defeat in his voice when he'd wanted to run away—from life, from me.

" *. . . Just remember in the winter,*
far beneath the winter snows,
lies the seed that, with the sun's love,
in the spring
becomes the rose."

I felt as if I was going to explode. 'I don't think I can live with this pain', I silently screamed. Shane is gone, gone forever, and all I have is the promise that the seed of hope I planted within him will guide him.

That's not good enough! I want him back!

Then my mind pushed the sadness away. Who picked this song? No one, not even James, knew the significance of this song to Shane and me. I felt invaded until I realized that Shane had sent it. Only he would know the power and impact it would have on me. Sadness fell over me. He was such a large part of my life, how was I to live without him?

By this time we were standing up ready to leave, and James was holding me. My knees were shaking and I was weak with emotion. An elderly Sioux woman standing directly in front of me turned around. She took James's free hand and shook it. Then she took my hand and held it, staring intently into my eyes. "I'm Shane's grandmother," she declared.

This woman was his *paternal* grandmother. I was speechless and couldn't break away from her piercing stare. Her eyes reflected lifetimes of her people, in a matter of seconds. As James began shuffling out of the pew, she broke the trance she held over me and nodded towards him. She indicated that I was holding up the line exiting the chapel. We were led across the street to the cemetery.

The priest blessed the grave with tobacco while six men beat ceremonial drums and wailed chants. It became a screaming contest between the priest and the drummers. The priest was ignored and pushed aside by the crowd (actually he was drowned out by the sound), while the drum continued to beat. The drums vibrated the earth, and began to comfort me. Others began to sob hysterically, and Missy ran off into the fields. This time she couldn't catch my attention. Shane's people were setting him free. As the drummers continued to chant, a flock of swallows flew off into the west, and I had a sense of a caged eagle being released from captivity. He was finally at peace.

156

14

Questions Unanswered

THE TRIP BACK TO MINNESOTA WAS LONG, BORING, AND VERY quiet, each of us immersed in our own thoughts. My friends' request to have a service continued to haunt me. I just didn't know if I had the energy to go through it all again. It would be inconvenient, uncomfortable, and I didn't want to take care of any more people. Then I began thinking about the loss they were feeling and how much they loved him, and I felt guilty. I still didn't want to do it, so I tried to push it to the back of my mind.

The suicide notes that Shane had left were addressed to Allana and Geri. He simply said goodbye and asked them not to be angry with him. Hoping that he might have left answers to all our questions, and secretly wishing he had thought of me before he died, I was very disappointed. I had anticipated that the letters might alleviate some of the pain. Instead, it made it worse.

The next three days were a nightmare. I thought about Shane constantly, wondering where he was, how he wanted to be remembered, and feeling deep guilt for not having been with him on his birthday. Actually, that was the only thing I felt guilty about. I knew that I had done everything in my power to help him. I was angry, though, with the tribe for wasting his life. Maybe if his people had intervened when he was a child, his terrible pain and suffering could have been prevented. I was angry with the JD Camp for not pushing foster care when he was in his deep depression. I was also still angry with Marlina for the torture she had made him endure.

Maybe things would have been different if he had lived with me again—but I knew there hadn't really been a chance of that. The revised Indian Child Welfare Act[1] forbade the fostering of Native American children by people of other races.

During the time between Shane's first suicide attempt and the actual event, his sense of spirit was extinguished. I blamed it on the anti-depressants and his frustration over finding a suitable foster home. According to Richard Heckler, author of *Waking Up, Alive: The Descent, the Suicide Attempt, and the Return to Life*[2], Shane was in a trance-like state, which Richard defined as "a narrowing of perception in which one fixates on one's pain and can imagine no future." Heckler stated, "If you can't imagine the future being any different, then suicide seems a logical option to stop the pain." Trying to practice empathy with Shane, I tried to imagine how he felt in the psych ward, having survived his hanging. Did he feel like a failure, or was he relieved that he was alive? As one suicide survivor recalled, "Now I'm in this no man's land of having my life back. But what do I do with it?"[3]

Shane felt that he was on the outside, looking in..., and this is a feeling shared by many suicidal people. Feelings of alienation can be intensified by racism, according to suicidal experts. I also attest to that fact, based on the discrimination Shane and I both felt due to our differences in skin color. In reflecting back to when I was a teenager, conformity among my peer group was rewarded. Cultural differences or individuality was perceived as inadequacy. The peer group isolated the teenager, and a cauldron of emotions festered within the body and mind of the teen.

This society, in general, has not welcomed, and in fact, fears adolescence. The adolescent, meanwhile, struggles with the paradoxical developmental stage of becoming an individual, yet trying to remain connected with others. I tend to agree with Richard Heckler, that "...it's hard to commit suicide when you feel connection."[4] And, a report from the American Association of Suicidology[5] concurs with this. Among Native Americans, the lowest rate occurs in communities with the greatest number of intact traditional religious clans and extended family structures.

Shane was caught between two worlds—his culture and the white culture. He loved big city life, but, whenever he spent any length of time in the city, he'd become agitated and get into trouble. But, upon returning to the reservation he eventually got bored, and found that the slower paced lifestyle didn't suit him. He had such a hard time fitting in anywhere and truly believed that having a supportive family would ease his confusion. Unfortunately, it did not. This child struggled with the issues faced by many Native Americans; how to live in both worlds without compromising his dignity, how to maintain humility, accept responsibility, and incorporate a spiritual base in the earthly realm. He continually flipped back and forth from the reservation to the city, the city to the reservation, desperately hoping to find peace and contentment. Where did he belong?

I, too, was searching to fulfill a preconceived notion of what an adult was and how an adult operates at work, at play, and at rest. As part of the Baby Boomer generation, I focused on accumulating material possessions and living a glamorous life of parties, drinking until all hours of the night, and climbing up the ladder of success. I had it all; fast car, condominium, the nightlife of the Twin Cities, career. Whatever I set my mind upon, I accomplished.

The reality is, even today, in this age of the enlightenment, people fear talking about suicide. For some bizarre reason, humans fear it might be contagious, or force the suicidal person to think about 'it'; thus forcing the person to commit the act. I have counseled hundreds of children and teenagers who have attempted suicide. The words which have reached them is by stating the obvious, "I believe you." These three simple words have broken down the most defiant, antagonistic teenager. How can we say we care about these children, yet not discuss feelings of hopelessness, loneliness, and fear of being viewed as a crazed lunatic?

Before teenager Paul Eppinger took his life, he wrote, "All I know, is that the few times I have truly touched and been touched by another person - those few times when I have really seen, and likewise been acknowledged as a reality and not a projection - the reward, the pure exhilarating freshness, was unmistakable."[6]

Did Shane hate life? Did he resent those who had it better than himself? Absolutely not! His laugh, his smile could brighten up the darkest room, his eyes had a brilliance that shone through to his soul. So how can it make any sense...if he didn't hate life, why did he end it? According to Stephen Levine[7], "People don't kill themselves because they hate life as much as they kill themselves because the love they have for life is not requited". I truly believe that if Shane had found a way to stop the pain he felt, he would not have taken his life.

Miller Newton, Ph.D., author of *Adolescence: Guiding Youth Through Perilous Ordeal*[8] believes that "suicide has risen dramatically in the past few decades because drugs have become more accessible to teens. 85% of all adolescent suicides are drug-and alcohol-related, but this may be overlooked because the suicide frequently occurs after the full effect of the drug has worn off." I will never know if or how much Shane was drug influenced before his suicide, but his history could not eliminate this question.

Another question remained. How much did Shane's abuse as a child contribute to his suicidal tendencies? His abusive history directly contributed to his lack of appropriate coping skills, distance from nurturance, and unresolved pain. Richard Heckler[9] explains, "If we eliminated or halved the amount of child abuse in this country, the suicide rate would drop precipitously." Shane continually returned to his mother only to suffer at her hands. If this relationship could have been reconciled, could it have prevented his death? Her death?

The spirit I shared with Shane was restless. I talked to him daily but could not find peace. Under EagleHeart's guidance, I made the decision to hold a pipe ceremony with the people who had been involved in Shane's life in the Twin Cities; the other half of his life, the white world.

I thought of various areas to hold the ceremony; parks and lakes where Shane and I visited, Mounds Park in St. Paul, where Native tribes were buried centuries past. I got in the car and drove to the bluffs overlooking the Mississippi River. Letting my heart lead the way I discovered burial mounds similar to the location at Mounds Park, with a circle of stones enclosing a fire pit. Surrounded by large oak trees with a vista of the river, I knew this was the place.

I visited the site the morning of the ceremony. It was cold and rainy, the trees barren of their leaves. I walked along the cliffs of St. Paul and thought about Shane's difficult life. His body and mind had become tired—tired of the pain, frustration, and unmet needs accumulated in his seventeen years. His future as an adult looked grim and he knew it. Without his mother, he would never have been able to receive the affirmation of love he needed from her. Even though I loved him, I couldn't give him Marlina's love.

The winds picked up.

I held the ceremony on October 20th. Shane's beadwork, which encircled the pipe stem, identified the four directions of the wind through color: red for the east, yellow for the south, black for the west, and white for the north. Two fragile seashells hung from the pattern. On the fringes of the pipe stem jingle beads held two feathers—one given to me by a Blackfoot woman from her ceremonial buckskin dress, and the feather I had found at the priest's house just before Shane's funeral.

I invited friends who had known him, some of whom had not known he died until I called about the ceremony. Krissy came with an Inuit family, a mother with four children, whom Shane had befriended while working at the shelter. Some of the staff from the women's' shelter, along with Barbara and Natalie, attended. James and Tara were there, of course, along with Robert and Joyce. Fourteen people—adults and children arrived at the Indian Mounds on the east side of St. Paul.

I had never led a pipe ceremony before, but knew that whatever I did, as long as it was offered with respect, would be acceptable. We gathered in a semi-circle around the unlit fire pit surrounded by trees. Everyone was nervous; only one other person had attended a pipe ceremony before. I acknowledged the four directions, offering kinnic kinnick each time. After loading the pipe with the tobacco, I placed it onto Mother Earth, the stem facing the sky. This moment acknowledged his passing, and many of the mourners began to weep.

I recited a poem that I had discovered during my first year working with abused children. It seemed perfect for Shane's epitaph:

Your children are not your children;
They are the sons and daughters
of life's longing for itself.

They come through you but not from you,
And though they are with you
yet they belong not to you
You may give them your love but not your thoughts...

...For life goes not backward nor tarries with yesterday.

The Prophet, Kahlil Gibran[10]

We conveyed our anger, fears, confusion, and sadness with each other. I wondered if Shane was listening to this. Hearing people talk about emotions had always been difficult for him. As if he had read my thoughts, the four children started pulling at me, distracting me, and interrupting the adults who were talking.

Smiling, James said, "I think Shane's here all right, next to Deb, and he's telling the kids to distract her so she doesn't get so serious about this."

I stared at the children, who were crossing their eyes and sticking their tongues out at me, and one of them shouted, "That's right, Debbie!" I took the hint. We shared a feast of nurturing foods while we reminisced and laughed about the good times we had spent with Shane. It was a beautiful way to complete his time with us and send him onto his next journey.

Two eagles helped me through this journey—EagleHeart and Shane Lone Eagle. Without their help I wouldn't have been able to lead Shane to his home. I'm very privileged to have helped celebrate my son's passing.

15

Epilogue

IT'S TAKEN ME QUITE A FEW YEARS TO FINISH SHANE'S LIFE STORY. During major life changing events, it often times takes years for the mind to process the information it learned, and the heart to heal the wounds left in the aftermath. It was a very difficult decision for me to write about such an intimate experience. I didn't want to exploit a tragedy, yet something very significant happened to me, and I wanted to share that perspective. Throughout the time Shane was in my life, I operated from a place of unconditional love, and even though I struggled in learning exactly what this type of love entailed, Shane would not accept any other type of love. As a child, I didn't learn about unconditional love from my family. I did learn that love had many conditions intertwined with it. I remember telling friends, in frustration, that this 'unconditional love stuff' sucked, and felt resentful that I didn't get anything in return except emptiness from Shane. In retrospect, I was very wrong in that summation.

My other hesitation in having this information in written form was the pain and sadness it resurrected within me. I was torn between sharing the intimate details or keeping the information to myself—like a secret that no one else needed to know. As I delved deeper into myself, I acknowledged that I was fearful of my emotions bursting through the dam that I had built around my heart. What was I afraid of? Success? Failure? Rejection? I feared that my anger and frustration at his death would scream out of the pages, alienating everyone who read it. I also feared that emotions would engulf me so deeply that I would lose my sense of self, forever. In the end, with the encouragement of many individuals, both friends and strangers, I realized that what I learned could help others in their lives. That's when I knew Shane's life needed to be made public.

Could I truly describe the journey I embarked on with mere words? Ironically, my career path consisted of listening to words; words of sorrow, angst, and pain, and yet the lack of the specific word to describe my relationship with Shane continued to perplex me. In my search I discovered a poem which aptly described both my frustration with language and in easing the pain of Shane's emotional wounds:

WORDS FOR IT

*I wish I could take language
And fold it like cool, moist rags.
I would lay words on your forehead.
I would wrap words on your wrists.
"There, there," my words would say
Or something better.
I would ask them to murmur,
"Hush" and "Shh, shh, it's all right."
I would ask them to hold you all night.
I wish I could take language
And daub and soothe and cool
Where fever blisters and burns,
Where fever turns yourself against you.
I wish I could take language
And heal the words that were the wounds
You have no names for.*

J.C. (The Artists Way, Julia Cameron[1])

The healing process after the loss of a loved one is slow. It crawls at a snail's pace, stopping to rest periodically, and just when you think it's finally over—another wave of grief topples you to the ground. I endured my loss as I was ending a very successful professional career, traveling around the country, meeting new friends, experiencing alternative ways of interacting with people. Years later, here I am, at the beginning of another fork in my life path, departing from a well-worn foot trail.

In Hawaii, it's very common for families to informally adopt children from other homes and raise them as their own. This occurs for many reasons; financial, spiritual, and emotional. It's called 'Hanai'. It alleviated stress for the biological family, and allowed the hanai child to be raised in an environment more adaptable to the child's well-being. From my observations, this system has worked well within the Hawaiian culture. When people ask if I have children, I automatically say no. How can I explain the love, the strong spiritual bond I had with Shane, a stranger's son? I occasionally tell acquaintances what happened, but they haven't understood my feelings. They usually minimized my loss, exclaiming, "He wasn't really your child, though, was he?"

I can't say whether the emotions I experienced were the same as those of someone losing a biological child, I have nothing to compare it with, but there is a deep scar on my heart.

I had thought that if I could have saved his life my mission on earth would have been fulfilled. And I had failed. Miserably. I was embarrassed to admit Shane had died, it reflected failure onto me. Yes, I took it personally. I assumed responsibility where I had no business assuming. How could I have saved another person's life when I barely saved my own? Where did I ever get the notion that I could control and direct another person's life? Shane mirrored the issues that I was trying so desperately to escape. Abandonment, issues with mother, fear of adulthood. Both of us longed to have a normal family, but I couldn't make it happen for Shane just as I couldn't force my own family to be normal.

The Native American culture and spirituality has become very popular in the non-native world, specifically white people have taken various aspects of the culture and have incorporated into their own lives. It's common to see artifacts from the Native American culture in homes across the United States and overseas. I question, though, if these avid collectors of art realize how the culture, as a whole, is struggling to survive. Shane's experience was not uncommon, life is very difficult for reservation children and children living off the reservation. Apathy is the norm for many of the children and teenagers. When we glean the positive qualities off of a culture, do we have a responsibility to also learn about the struggles that particular culture may be experiencing? For those who participate in sweat lodges, who vision quest for the spiritual knowledge and growth, is there an implied responsibility that goes along with the attainment of spirituality? As an example, many Americans who practice Tibetan Buddhism have studied the struggles of the Tibetan people and pray for the survival of the Tibetan culture.

This spiritual dilemma helped me to keep a humble and respectful focus throughout my writing. I represented only myself, my thoughts, and experiences.

As a product of the Baby Boomer generation, I invested a large amount of energy into my education and career. While working full time, I obtained a Bachelor's degree in child development and business management, and a Master's degree in child sexual abuse and feminist business management. I worked as a secretary (fulfilling my mother's expectations), a children's advocate at a battered women's shelter, a children's therapist, an assistant director for a domestic abuse therapy agency, a psychotherapist, a supervisor for a child abuse prevention program, and a lecturer at two colleges.

What I didn't find in my pursuit for knowledge and helping others was my spirit. Do we find this elusive spirit within ourselves? Praying in a church on Sundays? Offering financial contributions as a way of alleviating guilt? Or do we find it in other humans? If we go along with the premise that everyone around us reflects the strengths and weaknesses we have within ourselves, then what does that say about how we live our lives? What was Shane mirroring to me? Chaos, confusion, mistrust, dysfunction, drama. But also the childlike qualities I had lost; the happiness of laughing, being silly, and brief moments of pure, boundless love.

One particular trip, returning from a vision quest in South Dakota, three women and myself were discussing our search for teachers of spirituality. I was under the illusion that a teacher would appear, ready to teach me about the mysteries and life-challenging questions of the world. These women, too, had searched unsuccessfully for that elusive master. We reviewed the people who influenced our lives and speculated whether our generation would have designated teachers for us. I began to feel uneasy and contemplated whether I was destined to have a specific person or numerous masters threaded throughout my lifetime, teaching me to become a teacher for future generations.

As Sandy Boucher, author of *Opening the Lotus: A Woman's Guide to Buddhism*[2] suggested, "... some of us must become the teacher we have always wanted to find." Sandy explained how to accomplish this, "Women choose to practice on their own or with minimal involvement of a teacher, perhaps in circles of like-minded men and women and families."

I continued to question who my master might be, attending workshops and conferences of various spiritual leaders. Unbeknownst to me, I was introduced to my spirit and it's guide during the most tumultuous and chaotic time in my life—and I pleaded ignorance.

The eagle continued to haunt my dreams, shape shifting into Shane then returning to it's original form. The eagle repeatedly begged me to enter the Spirit World with him. Sobbing in my sleep, I cried out that I couldn't leave, and the eagle flew off into the distant night sky. This was a reoccurring dream and each time the eagle became more impatient with me. The days were wrought with memories and I felt trapped in a cold, empty void. I wanted to talk to Shane, hear his voice, touch his face, I missed him to the point of unbearable pain. I kept an impenetrable concrete wall around my grief. Friends praised me, "You're so brave and strong. I really admire you."

If they only knew they were actually encouraging me to remain cold and distant. I desperately needed spiritual guidance and when the opportunity for vision quest in South Dakota presented itself, I knew I had to participate. I hoped to communicate with Shane in the spirit world, and explain why I couldn't join him. I also yearned to know if he had taken his unresolved problems into the spirit world and needed my assistance. Perhaps his need for a mother figure was so strong that it drove him to re-enter the physical realm, calling me to him. The temptation to join him was great, the loneliness and heart ache was unbearable, but I knew it wasn't my time.

I decided to make a list of questions for the vision quest, and when the time was appropriate, ask Shane. I wasn't sure how he would answer me, but the haunting had to stop, I was now seeing images of him during the daylight hours.

The vision quest was organized for late in the Fall season, and the threat of snow turned into reality with plunging temperatures of 12 and 15 degrees. The thought of sitting outside, in the snow, made me reconsider my decision, and others in the group were also backing out of the trip. Two days before the scheduled date, the weather stabilized and we decided to go ahead with our plans. I pulled my travel bag packed with wool sweaters, mittens and rain gear, out of my dad's truck. He had given me a ride to the church from which we would carpool the 450 miles. Four women and two men, who hadn't met each other before that day, headed west toward the Black Hills and Spirit Mountain. We exchanged passengers during the thirteen hour drive and made frequent stops to break the monotony. There was a sense of anticipation in the air.

We began a two day fast which would continue until we came down from the mountain. I had brought my peacepipe, sage, sweetgrass, and kinnickinnick for ceremonial ritual. Taking an inventory of the items in my duffle bag, EagleHeart suddenly broke my thoughts. "Geez, I forgot my sleeping bag. I can't believe it!" Staring at him, I flashed my mind to my down sleeping bag, sitting on the hallway floor, 300 miles away.

"That makes two of us" I groaned, flashing to the vision of freezing in the cold, bitter wind, perched on the side of the mountain top. We stared at each other in disbelief, shrugged our shoulders, and reassured ourselves by saying "How cold can it get up there anyway?"

We arrived at Rapid City in the early afternoon, EagleHeart wanted to stop by a friend's house to pick up a tarp for the sweat lodge. His friend, Chokeberry, greeted and welcomed us into his home. I sat on the couch, next to a woman named Kris, directly facing our host. It was difficult to concentrate on the small talk because I was distracted by a blue haze floating above our heads. I glanced around, checking to see if anyone else noticed this phenomenon. The others were engrossed in Chokeberry's stories of spiritual conquest, so I focused on Chokeberry's forehead. Through my peripheral vision, I saw a snarling black bear with enlarged fanged teeth, glaring at me. Shaking my head, trying to clear the vision, I stared at the floral design in the carpet. Apprehensively, I directed my attention above Chokeberry's head and the vicious bear growled, snapping its extended claws at me. I cowered into the couch and glancing above me, saw a eagle circling my head, cackling at the bear. It's wings were extended, ready to attack the bear. The rest of the group had a mesmerized, faraway look in their faces with no comprehension of the power struggle between the spirits of Chokeberry and myself.

Chokeberry was very animated, dominating the conversation. As he reestablished eye contact with me, the bear attacked the eagle. The bear tearing and ripping the eagle's wings; the eagle hissing and clawing at the bear's bloodied eyes. As quickly as the vision started, it dissolved. Flushed and sweating, I stared into Chokeberry's eyes. He smiled sardonically at me, stood up, and graciously led the group on a tour of his home. I remained behind, shaken by the magnitude of violence the vision had brought to me. Whoever this Chokeberry was, I wanted to leave his house quickly and never return. I purposefully didn't mention my shamanic vision with EagleHeart, I wanted to process it during the vision quest.

As we approached the turnoff for Spirit Mountain, a young golden eagle flew directly in front of the car. The mountain stood alone in a lush valley of wilderness, covered with green pine trees and surrounded by grasslands. Standing at five thousand feet, it was majestic against the backdrop of the flatlands of South Dakota. Buffalo roamed freely around the circumference of the mountain, protected by a wildlife refuge. We followed a foot trail leading towards it's base. Red, yellow, black, white, blue and green ribbons of material flickered in the wind, wrapped around trees, shrubs, and rocks. It was a beautiful acknowledgment of the four directions, Father Sky, and Mother Earth. It reminded me of the religious statues in church, but, unlike the cold rigidity those statues reflected, the colors fluttered through the air like ballet dancers, gently caressed by the winds.

The trail ended at three various sized sweat lodges. EagleHeart explained that the lodges were built by the surrounding tribes in the area. The women began covering the Sioux built lodge with tarps while the men built a fire to heat the stones. While the sun set to the west in a quiet and serene setting, a full moon rose from the east, with a brilliant iridescent glow. We prepared tobacco tie offerings, which are another form of prayer, under the incandescent moon. The offerings were made by placing a pinch of kinnickinnick in a square-shaped cloth; the specific color of the cloth represents one of the four directions. The four corners were then gathered and tied into four or seven bundles.

The eagle appeared to me for the second time, during the sweat lodge's last endurance. Sensing my sadness over the death of Shane, the eagle spoke, "Don't be sad, it was the way it should have been. I have lived my destiny."

"Hetch etu aloh. It is so, indeed", I answered. The eagle slowly faded.

Layering in long underwear, two wool sweaters, scarf and mittens, I, along with EagleHeart and Kris selected a trail which led to the mountain's summit. Not accustomed to hiking at higher altitudes, I climbed the fifteen steps to an observation landing at the halfway point, huffing and puffing. Stretched out on the deck, we stared up into the star-studded, cloudless sky.

"Look up there, is that the Big Dipper?" I gestured with my finger, pointing to a constellation.

"How'd you do that?" EagleHeart yelled out.

"Do what?"

"With your finger," he gestured, "Hold your finger up again."

I raised my arm towards the sky and pointed my finger.

"My God, Kris!" he cried out, "Did you see that? Look!"

I started getting frightened. "What's going on?" I screamed.

"There's a greenish-white light streaming from you fingertips. Hold up your other fingers. See? Draw something in the sky."

I drew a circle.

EagleHeart described the apparition. "The light's spraying out of your finger and drawing the image into the sky. Like chalk on a blackboard." He then pointed his finger up and drew a figure in the sky. He stopped and the image remained for a few seconds. We then put our hands together and aimed our fingers towards the sky. Light showered into the sky and we held the position until our arms ached. Knowing we had a long night ahead of us, we broke the spell and continued our ascent.

"Here Deb, take this for me, okay?" Eagleheart asked.

Without glancing at it, I took a small bag and stuffed it into my bag. We hiked a short distance together until I spotted a narrow ridge jutting out of the blackness.

"See you tomorrow!" I called back, and hiked up a rocky hill toward the peak.

Surveying the area, I dropped my bag next to a miniature pine tree, stunted by the high altitude winds. My site overlooked all directions except the west. Extremely strong winds knocked me down, and forced me to crawl on my hands and knees, posting protection colors at each of the four directions. I set up camp within this protection area, which took only a few minutes. I tried to pull out my peacepipe but it was caught. After a few tugs a plastic bag jumped out. It was the bag EagleHeart had given me. Checking inside, red blue and green swatches of material were rolled into a tube and tied with masking tape.

I remembered Chokeberry handing something to EagleHeart as we were driving off, and realized this was it. I debated whether I should toss it over the cliff, but I focused on it's intent. EagleHeart believed that women have strong spirit, and I think he wanted to help Chokeberry by giving the bundle to a woman. I offered the colors up to the spirit world and sensed sickness and possible death to a female relative that Chokeberry deeply loved. I prayed to Wakan Takan, the Great Spirit, that only positive energy be brought forth from the colors and the prayers of Chokeberry be answered in a positive manner.

Epilogue

The wind howled relentlessly, with gusts knocking me over. I was so cold I was shaking uncontrollably, teeth chattering, and the night had just begun. I hunted for more clothes, I wouldn't last the night at this rate. Wearing every piece of clothing and putting the duffle bag around my mittens, the bulkiness hindered my movement. I was becoming obsessed with the cold so I decided the wisest thing to do was sleep, then the wind and cold wouldn't affect me.

I stared into the clear, midnight blue sky. My mind wandered to James and I psychically sent him a message that I was safe. I thought of my friends, sleeping in their warm beds, while I was freezing. I felt like I should be doing something, and began to get angry at EagleHeart. Like a typical washichu[3] (white man) I wanted explicit instructions, expectations laid out, and guidelines explained. I had expected to be entertained with supernatural events every second spent in vision quest. I was disappointed.

And bored. After a few minutes of ranting and raving, I realized I had all the instructions I needed, the rest was up to me. Facing west I turned my back to the wind. The icy cold gusts rocked my body, I tried to resist the force to no avail. I gave up and the wind flipped me over onto my back. My face was exposed and was so stiff from cold it ached to move my eyes. Exhausted, I tried to meditate and eventually dozed off until I was startled by movement directly beneath me. I felt it through my clothes, a round, hard object in the small of my back. Snake popped into my mind, but I knew no animal or reptile would be stupid enough to be in this exposed wind. I opened my eyes and felt someone standing directly behind my head. As I contemplated my next move, the object under my back began to move up towards my shoulders and away from my body. I shifted my eyes to the right and saw a rock the size of a golf ball rolling away from me. Terror filled my body while an inner voice screamed, "MOVE AWAY, NOW."

I jumped up, grabbed my pipe and ran to a far corner of my protection area. I couldn't leave the site so my choices were limited. On the outskirts of the protection area was a small cove on the slope of the north ridge. I checked and rechecked the stability of the rocks beneath me as I settled in. I tried to burn Sage for protection, but the wind kept blowing the flame out.

My toes and fingers were the first appendages to succumb to the cold. My fingers throbbed with pain and began to swell. I tried meditation, visualization and imagery, to bring warmth into my body. I relived memories of sailing on Lake Superior on a hot sunny afternoon, basking in the steamy sun's rays. I dozed off for a few minutes until my shivering body woke me up. I tried one sitting position, then switched to another. I felt like a fish floundering around the bottom of a boat.

I heard rocks skipping along the slope below me. I speculated if these were the Thunder Eggs that Chokeberry had described. Rocks the size of tennis balls, resembling meteorites, skipped and rolled across the land, up mountains, crossing rivers, through prairie lands, with the mission of protecting and watching over the earth.

The east horizon began to lighten, ever so faintly. It was the longest and coldest night I had ever experienced. I watched a small area of sky begin to brighten and slowly spread, like cream poured into black coffee. I was fortunate to view the sunrise sitting on a holy vortex, and reflected on how many others before me were also inspired by this sight. I prepared for a sunrise ceremony, now oblivious to my discomfort. Pulling out my peace pipe, which had been loaded with kinnickinnick before the sweat lodge ceremony, I assembled the stem into the pipestone. Memories flashed before me of where the pipe had led me, from its conception to Shane's spirit ceremony.

A sliver of sun turned the sky into a brilliant gold. As I held the peace pipe in a ceremonial stance, a red-tailed hawk flew out of the mountain's shadows and crossed between the sun and sky. The hawk was followed by a black songbird chirping a morning greeting. The hawk circled the area directly above me, cawing out. I smoked my pipe, watching sparrows, ravens, and an occasional eagle dance in the sky. This is what life was meant to be, not the stress and tension I endured trying to exist in society.

I shared my reasons for vision questing to the Spirit World and Wakan Takan. I conversed freely, as if I were talking to my best friend. Sensing that Shane's spirit needed to be called forth, I beckoned him, with grief stricken thoughts enveloping me. A bird distracted my concentration, squawking a shrill cry. I followed the sound and a bird soared through the air in the near distance. The glare from the sun distorted it's shape, but it's gigantic wingspan movements echoed throughout the canyon walls. The squawking penetrated my being and began to take the form of thoughts.

"I am Shane's spirit, do not be afraid. I will always take the shape of eagle, unless it frightens you. I soar to beautiful worlds, many more than Mother Earth. I know you are sad, but I am free. I have been released from your soul. You must release me from your mind."

I had many questions to ask the eagle, and, reading my mind, he explained his perception. "I am safe in the Spirit World. I am accepted for who I am. I will go back to your world to continue with my lessons and complete karmic experiences from past lives. I will not return in physical form until my training is completed.

"When I think about my previous lives I become angry that I did not learn the lessons which are so obvious to me now. I do not regret taking my life. My spirit had been permanently scared. I would not have survived adulthood without losing my dignity.

"My mother and I are on different planes. I am not better than her. Her training is different from mine. She is as happy as she allows herself to be. I know this through my wisdom.

"I want you to be with me, but I understand that you must help others before you join me. You must understand, though, you can enter the Spirit World at any time. When you are spiritually and physically ready, I can take you, not before. I know this to be true. Do not fear my visits with you. I can take my old human form as you physically know me, or as my true form, eagle. I prefer eagle, but know my power frightens you. I do not choose to take my old form. It does not fit me anymore.

"I am proud you will write about me, your writings will show the light to humans who are troubled and release them from their pain. Write what I have told you. I want humans to understand the Spirit World and not fear it. Death is not to be viewed with fear."

As I watched the eagle soar towards the north, feelings of relief flowed through my body. I would survive. Even though I missed Shane and would continue to grieve, I knew he was safe. It was time to find my own path.

In the distance, I heard a friendly voice yell out, "Hey Deb, I'm heading down. You ready or do you want to stay up here a while longer?"

"I'm definitely ready. I just have to pack up. I'll meet you at the platform" I yelled in return. Offering tobacco as thanks to Wakan Takan, I hurried to catch up with EagleHeart.

My vision quest was an endurance in the physical and spiritual realms. Life allows us to practice vision questing through crises, tragedies, and disasters. The challenge is to remain aware throughout the tribulations thrown our way. Some people choose to pursue endurance through physical exercise, for example triathalons, kayaking across Lake Superior. Others quest in nature through hiking, fishing, camping. My endurance took a very unusual form, through another human being—a child. Gifts from the spiritual world are unobtrusive, subtle, and do not include instruction manuals. I received a gift that I was completely unaware of, but, true to the information on the vision quest, led me to another fork on my path, my continued search for a spirit guide.

Epilogue

For You

*For you I leave my dreams, wishes, and love
And no matter where I'm at
you're the one I'll be thinking of.*

*I love you with all my heart
But I'm sorry that we have to part.
What I am saying is not a lie,
Without you I would have died.*

*You will be with me wherever I go.
Just remember that I love you so
Wherever you go, I'll be there too*

*Just keep in mind that all of this
is
for you!*

Shane Lone Eagle

Found in Deborah's computer two months after his death.

Notes

Chapter One

1. Guillaume Apollinaire. 1880-1918, french poet, source unknown.
2. Gail Sheehy. *New Passages: mapping your life across time.* (New York: Ballantine Books, 1995), p. 38-43, copyright© 1995 by G. Merritt Corporation
3. _____. *New Passages: mapping your life across time.* (New York: Ballantine Books, 1995), p. 41, copyright© 1995 by G. Merritt Corporation
4. Black Elk. 1863-1950, Holy Man of the Oglala Sioux, source unknown.

Chapter Three

1. Ed McGaa. *Native Wisdom: Perceptions of the Natural Way.* (Mpls, Mn.: Four Directions Publishing, 1995), p. 236.
2. Ibid., p. 232

Chapter Four

1. Indian Child Welfare Act of 1978, Title 25, Chapter 21. Requires placement cases involving Indian children be heard in tribal courts and permits the children's tribe to be involved in state court preceedings. The law requires Indian children be placed with extended family members, other tribal members, or other Indian families.

Chapter Six

1. **The Rose,** by Amanda McBroom
   (C) 1977 Warner-Tamerlane Publishing Company Corp. and Third Story Music Inc. All Rights Administered by Warner-Tamerlane Publishing Corp.
   All Rights Reserved   Used by Permission
   WARNER BROS. PUBLICATIONS U.S. INC., Miami, FL 33014

Chapter Nine

1. Richard Bach. *Illusions.* (New York: Dell Publishing Co.), 1977.

Chapter Ten

1. Andrea Young Ward. *The Question of Life.* Common Boundary Magazine, Volume 14, Issue 4, July/August, 1996. p 32. Common Boundary Magazine, 5272 River Road, Suite 650, Bethesda, MD 20816.
2. Ibid., p. 30.
3. Ibid., p. 30.
4. Ibid., p. 31.
5. Carolyn S. Henry. (1995). A Human Ecological Approach to Adolescent Suicide. *The Prevention Researcher,* 3(3), pp. 1-5. *The Prevention Researcher* is published by Integrated Research Services, a nonprofit research and education corporation located at 66 Club Road, Suite 370, Eugene, OR 97401 (800) 929-2955 *or* via E-Mail at: lainteg@cerf.net.
6. Andrea Young Ward. *The Question of Life.* Common Boundary Magazine, Volume 14, Issue 4, July/August, 1996. p 32, Common Boundary Magazine, 5272 River Road, Suite 650, Bethesda, MD 20816.
7. Ed McGaa, Eagle Man. *Mother Earth Spirituality*: *Native American Paths to Healing Ourselves and our World.* (New York: HarperCollins, 1990), p. 137-145.

Chapter Eleven

1. Reubin Snake. *Being Indian Is ...* Pamphlet found in North Dakota trading post, 1995.
2. Hoberman, H. and Garfinkel, B. (1988). Completed Suicide in Youth. Canadian Journal of Psychiatry, 33, 494-504. *The Prevention Researcher,* 3(3), p 5-8. *The Prevention Researcher* is published by Integrated Research Services, a non-profit research and education corporation located at 66 Club Road, Suite 370, Eugene, OR 97401 (800) 929-2955 *or* via E-Mail at: lainteg@cerf.net.

Chapter Thirteen

1. **The Rose,** by Amanda McBroom
   (C) 1977 Warner-Tamerlane Publishing Company Corp. and Third Story Music Inc. All Rights Administered by Warner-Tamerlane Publishing Corp.
   All Rights Reserved   Used by Permission
   WARNER BROS. PUBLICATIONS U.S. INC., Miami, FL 33014

Chapter Fourteen

1. Indian Child Welfare Act of 1978, Title 25, Chapter 21. Requires placement cases involving Indian children be heard in tribal courts and permits the children's tribe to be involved in state court preceedings. The law requires Indian children be placed with extended family members, other tribal members, or other Indian families.
2. Andrea Young Ward. *The Question of Life.* Common Boundary Magazine, Volume 14, Issue 4, July/August, 1996. p 32.
   Common Boundary Magazine, 5272 River Road, Suite 650, Bethesda, MD 20816.
3. Ibid., p. 32
4. Ibid., p. 33
5. Ibid., p. 35
6. Ibid., p. 33

Chapter Fourteen-continued
7. Ibid., p. 32
8. Ibid., p. 34.
9. Ibid., p. 35
10. Kahil Gibran. *The Prophet*. (New York: Random House Publishers Inc., 1923), p. 18.

Chapter Fifteen

1. Reprinted by permission of Jeremy P. Tarcher, Inc. a division of the Putnam Publishing Group from the ARTIST'S WAY by Julia Cameron. Copyright © 1992 by Julia Cameron.
2. Sandy Boucher. *The Dance of Gender*. Adapted from *Opening the Lotus: A Woman's Guide to Buddhism*, Beacon Press, 1997. Shambhala Sun Magazine, July, 1997, Volume 5, Number 6, p. 25. 1345 Spruce Street, Boulder, CO 80302-4886.
3. Ed McGaa. *Native Wisdom: Perceptions of the Natural Way*. (Mpls, Mn.: Four Directions Publishing, 1995), p. 236.

Suggested Readings

The following authors have assisted me along my path; perhaps these books will also be of guidance for your journey:

Bradshaw, John. *Family Secrets, What You Don't Know Can Hurt You.* Bantom Book, 1995.
Lerner, Harriet G. *Dance of Intimacy.* Harper & Row, 1989.
Linnea, Ann. *Deep Water Passage, a spiritual journey at midlife.* Pocket Books, 1993.
Sheehy, Gail. *New Passages. Mapping Your Life Across Time.* Ballantine Books, 1995.
Wesselman, Hank. *Spiritwalker.* Bantom Books, 1995.

ADOLESCENT SUICIDE/GRIEF:

Eppinger, Charles and Eppinger, Paul. *Restless Mind, Quiet Thoughts: A Personal Journal.* White Cloud Press, 1994.
Heckler, Richard. *Waking Up Alive: The Descent, the Suicide Attempt, and the Return to Life.* Putnam Books, 1995.
Levine, Stephen. *Guided Meditations, Explorations and Healings.* Anchor Books, DoubleDay & Co., 1991.
Levine, Stephen. *Healing into Life and Death.* Anchor Books, DoubleDay & Co., 1987.
Levine, Stephen. *Meetings At The Edge.* Anchor Book, DoubleDay & Co., 1984.
Lewis, C.S. *A Grief Observed.* Bantam Books, 1961.
Marcus, Eric. *Why Suicide?* HarperSanFrancisco, 1996.
Newton, Miller.. *Adolescence: Guiding Youth Through the Perilous*

Ordeal. W.W. Norton & Co., Inc., 1995.

Orbach, Israel. *Children Who Don't Want To Live*. Jossey-Bass Publishers, 1988.

Slaby, Andrew, M.D. and Lili Frank Garfinkel. *No One Saw My Pain: Why Teens Kill Themselves*. W.W. Norton, 1994.

The Prevention Researcher, *The Prevention of Adolescent Suicide*. Fall, 1996, Vol 3, No. 3.

Ward, A.Y., *The Question of Life*. Common Boundary Magazine, July/August, 1996. pp 30-35.

Williams, Kate. *A Parents Guide for Suicidal and Depressed Teens*. Hazelden Foundation, 1995.

NATIVE AMERICAN STUDIES:

Brown, Joseph Epes. *The Sacred Pipe: Black Elk's Account of the Seven Sacred Rites of the Oglala Sioux*. Norman: University of Oklahoma Press, 1953.

Fire, John (Lame Deer) and Richard Erdoes. *Lame Deer Seeker of Visions*. New York: Simon & Schuster, 1972.

Johnson, Sandy and Dan Budnik. *The Book of the Elders*. San Francisco: Harper Collins, 1994.

Mails, Thomas. *Fools Crow*. Tulsa, OK: Council Oaks Books, 1991.

McGaa, E., Eagle Man. *Mother Earth Spirituality*. HarperCollins, New York, 1990

McGaa, E., Eagle Man. *Native Wisdom*. Four Directions Publishing Company, 1995.

McGaa, E., Eagle Man. *Rainbow Tribe*. HarperCollins, New York, 1992.

Neihardt, John G. *Black Elk Speaks*. New York: William Morrow, 1932. Reprint Lincoln: University of Nebraska Press, 1957.

Sandoz, Mari. *Crazy Horse: The Strange Man of the Oglalas*. Lincoln: University of Nebraska Press, 1961.

WOMENS STUDIES:

Arcana, Judith, *Our Mothers' Daughters*. The Women's Press, LTD., 1992.
Davenport, Kiana. *Shark Dialogues*. Penguin Books, 1994.
Douglas, Susan. *Where the Girls Are*. Times Books, 1995.
Lindbergh, Anne Morrow. *Gifts From the Sea*. Random House, 1955.
Pinkola Estes, Clarissa. *Women Who Run With the Wolves*. Ballentine Books, 1992.

ABOUT THE AUTHOR

Deborah Chavez, M.A. is a psychotherapist and a college lecturer who has specialized in the area of child abuse/neglect for the past fourteen years, and works in the field of eating disorders. She teaches courses in psychology, human development, and women studies at Hawaii Community College and lectures at the University of Phoenix.

Deborah, a minister of the Tenrikyo religion, a mind-body system of belief based in Japan, has also studied and utilizes the ancient Hawaiian Ho'oponopono process; and was a student of the Diamond Work Approach.

A contributing author to *Mother Earth Spirituality* by Ed McGaa Eagleman (HarperCollins, 1990), she lives with her husband Alan, two dogs named Kukui and Leilani, and one cat named Kitty, on the flanks of an active volcano on the Big Island of Hawaii . . . and appreciates every day of life in paradise!

Deborah offers workshops, consultations, and spiritual counseling. For more information or to share comments on *Fallen Feather*, please contact the author at:

Deborah Chavez
PO Box 4434
Kailua-Kona, HI 96745
email: dchavez@ ilhawaii.net

Fallen Feather
Order Form

If you would like to order additional books at $11.00, please complete the following:

Please send me:

_____ books

Total book cost $_____
plus $1.00 shipping per book: $_____
for a total of: $_____

(Include check or money order. Please remit in U.S. funds.)

_____
Name

_____
Address

_____
City/State/Zip Code   (Country, if outside USA)

Four Directions Publishing Company
C/O Northwestern Press
1017 Front Avenue
St. Paul, MN 55103
(612) 488-0523